From Discrimination to Inclusion

From Discrimination to Inclusion

A Journey of Transforming and Embracing Diversity

Ruth Chu-Lien Chao

LEXINGTON BOOKS
Lanham • Boulder • New York • London

Published by Lexington Books
An imprint of The Rowman & Littlefield Publishing Group, Inc.
4501 Forbes Boulevard, Suite 200, Lanham, Maryland 20706
www.rowman.com

86-90 Paul Street, London EC2A 4NE

British Library Cataloguing in Publication Information Available

Library of Congress Cataloging-in-Publication Data Available

ISBN 978-1-66694-649-9 (cloth : alk. paper) | ISBN 978-1-66694-650-5 (ebook)

∞™ The paper used in this publication meets the minimum requirements of American National Standard for Information Sciences—Permanence of Paper for Printed Library Materials, ANSI/NISO Z39.48-1992.

Contents

Preface

Two hundred years after the American Revolution, it is evident that some individuals still view the world through a racial lens. Historically, discussions surrounding racial discrimination have often centered on its impact on racial minority groups within society. Psychologists have extensively studied the clinical significance of racism and its profound effects on the psychological well-being of these minority populations. However, it is essential to recognize that racism also harms White individuals. Racism, in all its forms, is traumatic for anyone exposed to it, causing various types of harm to different groups. It is deeply ingrained throughout our society and culture. Even a system founded on White supremacy ultimately harms not only Black, Indigenous, and People of Color (BIPOC) but also White individuals. For instance, some White individuals may experience a phenomenon known as "White fragility." This term refers to the discomfort White individuals may feel when engaging in discussions about racism.

It's important to understand that what is often described as discomfort in White individuals during conversations about racism is, in fact, a trauma response. According to The National Alliance on Mental Illness, during the initial phases of a trauma response, people may struggle to process and stabilize when confronted with challenging information. This can result in emotional reactions such as frustration, anger, confusion, irritation, overwhelm, or numbness.

Given that discussions about racism may trigger traumatic responses in White individuals, this book aims to facilitate a transformation. It seeks to help White individuals move beyond their discomfort and embrace diversity, which can be a healing force. Embracing diversity has the potential to enhance creativity and encourage White individuals to seek out novel information and perspectives, ultimately contributing to better mental health.

Furthermore, embracing diversity allows individuals, including White people, to become more self-aware and gain an appreciation for cultural diversity. Understanding one another's backgrounds is essential for personal and community growth. Diversity enriches our world.

In light of the healing potential inherent in embracing diversity, this book will integrate strategies to help White individuals confront and challenge racism and address the traumatic responses that it can evoke. Through these efforts, it aims to foster a society where diversity is celebrated and racism is actively addressed for the benefit of all.

Introduction

Racial Discrimination vs. Racial Inclusion

Racial discrimination, tragically ingrained in American history, persists as a shadow that has evolved but never entirely dissipated. Its roots extend to the colonial period, with slavery establishing a foundation for centuries of racial inequality. Although the abolition of slavery was a significant turning point, it led to the era of Jim Crow laws, perpetuating racial segregation and discrimination. The Civil Rights Movement of the 1950s and 1960s, spearheaded by leaders like Martin Luther King Jr. and Rosa Parks, marked a critical fight against this systemic injustice, culminating in significant legal victories like the Civil Rights Act of 1964. However, the enduring effects of this tumultuous history continue to resonate in modern America.

A striking example is the ongoing racial disparities in police shootings. The issue of racial disparities in incarceration in the United States has been a long-standing problem that has persisted for many decades. While it's difficult to pinpoint an exact starting date for these disparities, they have been a significant concern since at least the mid-twentieth century and have continued to be a prominent issue in the criminal justice system. Several factors contribute to these disparities, including systemic racism, discriminatory policies, socioeconomic inequalities, and disparities in policing and sentencing. These disparities have been the subject of numerous studies, reports, and discussions in both academic and policy circles.

Although several reasons were causing the racial disparities in incarceration, in 2021, Black individuals, constituting 13 percent of the US population, accounted for 27 percent of those fatally shot by police. This statistic not only highlights persistent inequalities but also mirrors the troubling past. The journey from the era of slavery through the Civil Rights Movement has laid a complex groundwork for the current fight against inequality. Today's disproportionate police shootings of Black individuals are a stark reminder of this unfinished journey to racial equality. Understanding this deep-rooted history is essential in addressing the social and political challenges that continue to shape America's narrative on race and equality.

Despite numerous efforts to combat racism, including the landmark Civil Rights Movement, the struggle against racial discrimination persists in the United States. A poignant example of this ongoing battle is the tragic death of George Floyd in 2020. Despite the Civil Rights Act of 1964, which explicitly prohibited discrimination based on race, Floyd's death under the knee of a police officer for nine and a half agonizing minutes starkly reminds us that racial discrimination remains deeply entrenched in American society. From the Civil Rights Movement to the death of George Floyd, these events underscore the pervasive impact of racial discrimination, affecting both White individuals and people of color in profound and disparate ways.

Today, many people in the United States have heard about racial discrimination and various evidences to support the damage of racism; it is still a long road to help Americans heal from the trauma related to racial discrimination. Thus, having heard about racial discrimination is one thing; being able to recognize the damage of racial discrimination is quite another. In US history, racial discrimination has been a topic that has disturbed most people. People tend to avoid exploring and understanding racial discrimination. However, the more people avoid the issue of racial discrimination, the more unresolved impact it may have on us.

If racial discrimination is a topic that people avoid most, though it haunts people throughout history, the most critical question for us would be, "What is racial discrimination?" "Why does it cause people so many traumatic experiences?" An accurate definition of racial discrimination is inevitable because healing and reconciliation start with a clear definition. To know why racial discrimination hurts, we need to define and even redefine racial discrimination to align the meanings of racial discrimination with people's experiences.

DEFINITION OF RACIAL DISCRIMINATION

Racial discrimination refers to the differential and inequitable treatment of members of different ethnic, religious, national, or other groups. Racial discrimination indicates that members of these groups suffer or endure visible or invisible unfair treatment, which causes these members to struggle with psychological or emotional hardship. Discrimination is usually the behavioral, verbal, emotional, or psychological manifestation of prejudice and, therefore, involves negative, hostile, and dangerous treatment of rejected group members. Specifically, racial discrimination means that an individual is unequally treated because he/she/they come from a particular racial/ethnic background.

Racial discrimination could happen explicitly or implicitly because of personal characteristics associated with race (such as hair texture, skin color, or certain facial features). For example, assuming someone is a foreigner due to their accent or skin color. Specifically, color discrimination involves treating someone unfavorably because of skin color or complexion.

Since racial discrimination is an unjust treatment of individuals based on their race or ethnicity, it includes a range of behaviors and reactions, from overt acts of hatred and bigotry to subtle, implicit biases that create and exacerbate inequality. Racial discrimination, unfortunately, has not just happened randomly or recently. For example, Black people have been traumatized and brutalized by racial discrimination for at least hundreds of years. For members of racial/ethnic minority groups, racial discrimination has been experienced in their daily lives, school, workplace, society, culture, and history, in various formats such as interpersonal interactions, social media, and so on.

LEVELS OF RACIAL DISCRIMINATION

The levels of racial discrimination structure the definition of racial discrimination in this book. Indeed, racial discrimination can be manifested at different social levels. There are three purpose of structuring racial discrimination by levels. First, the levels of racial discrimination help explicitly explain that members of racial/ethnic minority groups live in a world entirely of racial discrimination, from individual interaction to policy. Second, the levels of racial discrimination demonstrate that racial discrimination is a nonstop, continuous, and ongoing traumatic experience perceived by members of racial/ethnic minority groups. Third, although it is a traumatic experience for members of racial/ethnic minority groups, the damage and hurts are shared and harmful for people across races and ethnicities, including the majority of Whites.

Level 1: Individual Racial Discrimination

Individual racism is often expressed through discriminatory actions, stereotypes, biases, and prejudices that individuals hold against others solely based on their race. It can manifest in various ways, including personal insults, hate speech, exclusionary practices, violence, and even microaggressions—subtle forms of discrimination that are unintentional but still perpetuate racial stereotypes and prejudices. This form of racism can be overt or covert, subtle or explicit, but regardless of the form it takes, it has detrimental consequences for both the individuals who experience it and society as a whole.

Individual racism means that someone adopts or accepts racist stigma, stereotypes, prejudice, or discrimination in their value or worldview. Individual racial discrimination may show someone's racist beliefs about members of racial/ethnic minority groups. Internalized racism refers to "a form of self-loathing based on the cognitive and emotional acceptance by individuals of an oppressed group of all or some aspects of the negative stereotypes" (Oxford University Press, 2024). Internalized racism is the process by which people internalize and accept the majority White culture's standard of appearance or beauty (Nittle, 2021). When someone identifies with negative or stereotyped assumptions against racial/ethnic minority groups, such identification may contribute to their lower psychological well-being and self-confidence. Internalized racism may also cause Black people's health problems, such as higher alcohol consumption, depressive symptoms, anxiety, and obesity (Willis et al., 2021). There is a variety of evidence showing that internalized racism damaged other racial/ethnic minorities' well-being, such as Asian Americans (Frisby, 2024; Kim et al., 2024) and Latino/as (Hipolito-Delgado, 2010; Mullany et al., 2022).

Interpersonal racism is another form of individual racial discrimination. Interpersonal racism occurs between individuals and includes explicit and implicit assumptions against racial/ethnic minority groups. Such assumptions impact individuals' interactions with members of these groups and may influence their interactions, behaviors, and perceptions toward others (Kornienko et al., 2022). Some examples are as follows but are not limited to:

- Salespersons or security personnel follow BIPOC shoppers, assuming they might steal stuff in the store.
- Attacks against or assuming Asian Americans for Covid or labeling Covid as a "China virus"
- Directly or indirectly suggests that immigrants steal jobs from Americans.
- Ask someone where they are from initially because of their accent.

Similar to internalized racism, interpersonal racism also destroys people's well-being and exacerbates psychological distress. Moreover, Nazroo, Bhui, and Rhodes (2020) found that "Black African people do face an increased risk of psychotic illness and an increased risk that is driven by racially based social and economic disadvantage, reflecting . . . interpersonal racism" (272). Although numerous studies report the harmful consequences of interpersonal racism on the psychological well-being of BIPOC, interpersonal racism hurts the majority of Whites as well. Wilson-Ahlstrom (2018) listed how racism harms White people. Interpersonal racism erases the personal connections between Whites and those BIPOC who are being hurt by the oppression and racism. Spanierman and Heppner (2004) found that racism may make Whites experience psychological costs such as guilt, anger, sadness, and helplessness.

Taken together, racism, starting at the individual level, has been a potent damaging the mental and emotional health of both BIPOC and Whites. In the fight against racism, neither BIPOC nor Whites are winners because we all get hurt. Without healing and racial inclusion, we are all losers in the war against racism.

Level 2: Institutional Racial Discrimination

Institutional racial discrimination is the next level of individual racial discrimination. According to the Encyclopaedia of Britannica (2024), institutional racism means "the perpetuation of discrimination based on 'race' by political, economic, or legal institutions and systems." Institutional racism significantly and negatively impacts the physical health and mental well-being of BIPOC. Braveman, Arkin, Proctor, and Holm (2022, 174) documented examples of the impacts of institutional racism. Racial discrimination has been a pervasive issue in society that has permeated various sectors, including (a) criminal justice systems, (b) educational institutions, and (c) workplaces. Taken together, the income disparity experienced by BIPOC communities can also be attributed to institutionalized racism, where policies, laws, and cultural norms perpetuate and legitimize racial inequalities. For instance, the criminal justice system disproportionately targets BIPOC individuals, leading to higher rates of incarceration and reduced employment prospects upon release.

Criminal Justice Systems. The criminal justice system, an institution designed to maintain law and order, often perpetuates racial disparities, resulting in unequal treatment and outcomes for BIPOC. Thus, it is critically important to analyze this issue by exploring the ways in which the criminal justice system perpetuates racism, the consequences of such racial bias, and potential solutions to rectify the systemic inequities.

The racism in criminal justice can be traced back to the brutal history of slavery, segregation, and systemic racism in the United States. This history has profoundly impacted the current structure and functioning of the criminal justice system. Laws such as the Black Codes, Jim Crow laws, and racially biased policing practices have all contributed to the disproportionately high rates of incarceration and mistreatment of people of color.

The disproportionate policing, punishment, and sentencing are another evidence of racism toward BIPOC in the criminal justice system. There is a glaring issue contributing to the perpetuation of racism within the criminal justice system: the disproportionate policing of BIPOC. Studies consistently demonstrate that law enforcement agencies are more likely to focus their efforts on neighborhoods with higher populations of people of color, resulting in the over-policing of these communities. Consequently, individuals from these communities are more likely to be arrested and targeted by law enforcement, regardless of whether they have committed more crimes than their White counterparts.

Moreover, racial bias in sentencing is evident when examining disparities in conviction rates, lengths of sentences, and rates of parole release. Studies have indicated that people of color, particularly African Americans and Hispanics, are more likely to receive harsher sentences compared to their White counterparts for similar offenses. These disparities elucidate a profoundly ingrained bias within the criminal justice system, with individuals of color facing systemic discrimination even within the courtroom.

The racial disparities inherent in the criminal justice system have profound effects on both communities and individuals. Over-policing and excessive arrests lead to strained relationships between law enforcement agencies and communities of color, fostering a sense of resentment and mistrust. Confidence in the system's fairness diminishes, affecting the perception of justice, participation in civic life, and cooperation with law enforcement.

The racial bias in criminal justice significantly impacts BIPOC youths. Specifically, young people of color, particularly Black males, are disproportionately affected by discriminatory policing and sentencing practices, resulting in lost opportunities and compromised futures. Moreover, the pervasive nature of racial bias in the criminal justice system perpetuates a cycle of incarceration, where individuals are labeled as criminals and face limited opportunities for rehabilitation, leading to high recidivism rates. Below are two examples of the criminal justice system's institutional racism.

Although people of color represent 39 percent of the US population, they make up over

Sixty percent of incarcerated people. A 2017 review noted that "nearly one in three black men will ever be imprisoned, and nearly half of black women currently have a family member or extended family member who is in prison." Approximately 1 in every 1,000 Black men is killed by police. Also, Black victims killed by police are more likely than White victims to have been unarmed, suggesting disparate treatment (p. 174).

However, the example of the criminal justice system, where BIPOC individuals make up 60 percent of the incarcerated population while only representing 39 percent of the US population, is merely the tip of the iceberg in terms of institutional racial discrimination. Institutional racial discrimination is everywhere in the lives of BIPOC, from living, healthcare, finance, and education.

Educational Institutions. Institutional racial discrimination also includes the disparities in education between White students and students of other racial/ethnic backgrounds. HBCUs are an example to explain the racism in education and the disparity of education received by Black students. Founded in the Civil War/Reconstruction era, HBCUs had a core mission of educating Black students to help them participate in the economy. Later, during the Jim Crow era, HBCUs educated the men and women who built Black communities and dismantled segregation (Alston et al., 2022). Recently, an initiative has been dedicated to a government-wide policymaking effort to eliminate barriers HBCUs face in providing the highest-quality education to a growing number of students (US Department of Education, 2023). Indeed, HBCUs offer all students an opportunity to develop their skills and talents regardless of race. These institutions train young people who serve domestically and internationally in the professions, as entrepreneurs and in the public and private sectors. Unfortunately, despite the significant contribution of HBCUs to US education, HBCUs are still underfunded. For example, more than one century since HBCUs were founded, America's historically Black colleges and universities have been vastly underfunded compared to those institutions that serve predominantly White students. Specifically, the government has financed the disparity between HBCUs and predominantly White institutions to be about $12.6 billion (McCray, 2023).

Education plays a crucial role in socioeconomic mobility, and disproportionate access to quality education is a key factor contributing to the income gap between BIPOC individuals and Whites. BIPOC communities often face inadequate funding, insufficient school resources, substandard infrastructure, and underqualified teachers, resulting in lower-quality education compared to predominantly White communities. Consequently, BIPOC students are less likely to have access to advanced courses, college preparatory programs, and, ultimately, prestigious higher education institutions. These educational disparities limit their future employment prospects, perpetuating the income gap.

Workplace. The workplace is another area significantly influenced by institutional racial discrimination. The workplace, arguably one of the most influential aspects of individuals' lives, is frequently characterized by institutional racial discrimination. This section aims to delve into the intricate facets of institutional racial discrimination in the workplace, focusing on the experiences faced by BIPOC employees and the impact it has on their opportunities for professional growth and overall well-being. It highlights the historical context, current challenges, and potential solutions to combat racial discrimination and promote equity in the modern workplace.

To understand the current challenges faced by BIPOC employees in the workplace, it is crucial to examine the historical backdrop that shaped these disparities. For Black people, the United States has a long-standing history of racial inequality, with centuries of slavery, followed by segregation and systemic marginalization of minorities.

Asian Americans, as early as 1862, were limited and not allowed to compete with White workers by imposing a tax on Asian Americans who attempted to work in manufacturing factories as well as on employers who hired Asian Americans. It was also intended to decrease immigration from Asian countries by reducing the number of jobs available (Kenny, 2023). These injustices in the workplace, whether historical or contemporary, have left a lasting impact on society, with BIPOC disproportionately affected in various aspects of life, including employment.

During the Jim Crow era, Black individuals were often relegated to low-wage jobs with limited opportunities for career advancement. Even after the Civil Rights Act of 1964 outlawed racial discrimination in employment practices, discriminatory practices persisted in subtler and more insidious forms, perpetuating racial disparities in the workplace. While overt racial discrimination in the workplace has become less common, institutionalized racial discrimination persists through implicit biases, systemic barriers, and tokenism. Microaggressions, biased performance evaluations, and biased hiring practices are subtle yet powerful obstacles that many BIPOC employees face.

Recruitment and hiring are another barrier for BIPOC in the workplace. Research shows that implicit biases, or unconscious biases held by individuals, can influence decision-making processes regarding hiring, promotion, and compensation. Individuals with non-European names, for instance, may encounter lower callback rates in job applications due to inherent biases. Implicit biases also contribute to limited opportunities for professional growth and advancement for racial minorities within organizations.

Systemic barriers, such as glass ceilings and limited access to mentorship and networking opportunities, further hinder BIPOC employees' progress. These barriers perpetuate inequalities by denying qualified workers opportunities to advance, resulting in missed talent and potential for both organizations and society.

Tokenism is another manifestation of institutional racial discrimination. It occurs when organizations hire a small number of minority employees to create an illusion of diversity while failing to address systemic issues that limit the opportunities for these employees to thrive. Tokenism hinders individual growth and prevents organizations from reaping the benefits of diverse perspectives and experiences, inhibiting innovation and progress.

The disparity in income between BIPOC and White people is another evidence of institutional racism in the workplace. The persisting income gap between BIPOC communities and Whites is a multifaceted issue rooted in historical, systemic, educational, and labor market dynamics. Recognizing and dismantling these institutional barriers is crucial for addressing this inequity. Unfortunately, income disparity remains a deeply entrenched issue within modern society, often correlating with various social and economic factors. When examining income inequality through the lens of race and ethnicity, it becomes apparent that BIPOC individuals consistently experience lower income levels compared to their White counterparts. This section aims to investigate the reasons behind this persistent income gap between BIPOC individuals and Whites, focusing on historical and systemic factors, educational disparities, discrimination, and labor market dynamics.

The income disparity between BIPOC individuals and Whites is deeply rooted in historical and systemic factors. These historical injustices have perpetuated a cycle of poverty and limited opportunities for BIPOC individuals, affecting their earning potential in the long run. Moreover, the differential access to capital, financial resources, and social networks further exacerbates the income gap and hinders economic advancement among BIPOC communities. Discrimination in the labor market is another significant factor contributing to the income disparity between BIPOC individuals and Whites. Various studies have demonstrated that BIPOC individuals face systemic biases throughout the hiring process, including racial profiling, unconscious bias, and stereotypes. These biases result in fewer job opportunities, limited access to managerial positions, and wage gaps across occupations.

Moreover, BIPOC individuals also tend to be concentrated in lower-paid industries and occupations, perpetuating the cycle of low incomes within these communities. Additionally, discriminatory housing practices, unequal access to credit and financing, and racial wealth gaps further contribute to the income discrepancy between BIPOC individuals and Whites. Moreover, it is reported that Black people and Latinos/as have significantly lower incomes than their White counterparts (Kochhar & Moslimani, 2023).

Level 3: Social Racial Discrimination

Racial discrimination at the societal level relates to the history of racism. To understand racism in our current society, it is inevitable to understand racism in the historical and contemporary contexts. Slavery, colonization, and segregation may be historical or forgotten terms by many people. However, the ongoing structural racism has perpetuated cycles of trauma and reinforced discriminatory beliefs. Today, racial profiling, microaggressions, police violence, and hate crimes contribute to the chronic exposure of marginalized communities to racism.

Racial discrimination is a deeply rooted societal issue that continues to plague even today's societies despite strides toward equality over hundreds of years. Racism at the social level refers to the unjust or prejudiced treatment toward BIPOC based on their race or ethnicity. It involves biases that limit opportunities, access to resources, social mobility, and the overall well-being of racial and ethnic minority populations. Discrimination can be overt, covert, systemic, explicit, or implicit, but its impact is pervasive, often leading to social disparities and perpetuating inequality.

To comprehend social racial discrimination, it is crucial to acknowledge its historical roots. Throughout history, societies worldwide have witnessed various forms of discrimination, such as slavery, colonization, apartheid, and segregation, which originated many years ago. These societal injustices have deeply influenced this country's systems and structures, perpetuating racial hierarchies that persist today. Understanding these societal foundations is essential to comprehend contemporary discriminatory practices as they shape inequalities.

The social level of racial discrimination includes stereotyping, prejudice, and microaggressions against BIPOC. Stereotypes and prejudices contribute significantly to social racial discrimination. Preconceived notions and generalizations about racial and ethnic minorities are often internalized and lead to biased treatment, both on individual and systemic levels. Microaggressions are subtle, everyday discriminations that occur in interactions, often unintentionally. These can include racial slurs, dismissive behavior, or colorblind racial statements, perpetuating power imbalances and contributing to a hostile environment for racial minorities.

Social and racial discrimination impose harsh and long-lasting consequences on individuals and communities. These effects permeate multiple aspects of life, including socioeconomic status, education, employment, health, and overall well-being. Discrimination can manifest in lower income levels, limited access to quality education, higher rates of unemployment, mental health issues, and adverse health outcomes. Moreover, societal divisions and tensions deepen, hindering social cohesion and obscuring progress toward a more inclusive society.

Many BIPOC individuals live in an environment that causes health disparities compared to their White counterparts. Environmental racism, a part of social racism, refers to the disproportionate exposure of racial and ethnic minority communities to hazardous environments and pollutants. These communities are often located near factories, waste disposal sites, or areas with inadequate clean air and water access.

Level 4: Media Racial Discrimination

The media plays a significant role in shaping public perception, often perpetuating stereotypes and biases. White individuals may also be subject to racial prejudice in the form of biased reporting or negative portrayals in the media. This can perpetuate cultural stereotypes, erode social cohesion, and foster a divisive social environment. Media is a powerful tool that shapes societies and influences public opinion. In recent years, racial discrimination has become a significant social issue. The media plays a crucial role in perpetuating racial discrimination by reinforcing stereotypes, promoting bias, and sustaining systemic inequalities through (a) reinforcement of stereotypes, (b) lack of representation, (c) prejudice and bias, and (d) amplification of systemic inequalities.

Reinforcement of Stereotypes. Media often perpetuates racial stereotypes, reducing complex individuals to one-dimensional caricatures. Such portrayals contribute to the stigmatization and marginalization of racial minority groups, reinforcing societal biases. For example, Asian Americans are often portrayed as cleaners in a clean shop or restaurant servers. Black people may be portrayed as criminals.

Lack of Representation. Racial discrimination in media is evident through the underrepresentation of minority groups. This exclusion perpetuates a cycle of invisibility and erases the diverse experiences and perspectives of people of color.

Prejudice and Bias. Racial discrimination portrayed in the media perpetuates prejudices and biases among its audience. Negative depictions can lead to the dehumanization of marginalized communities and contribute to a climate of hostility and discrimination.

Amplification of Systemic Inequalities. Media plays a significant role in amplifying and perpetuating existing systemic inequalities, such as racial disparities in employment, education, and criminal justice systems. Biased media coverage can reinforce these disparities and hinder progress toward racial equality and social justice.

In addition to the struggle with the media level of racial discrimination, there are four challenges regarding media racial discrimination. First, there needs to be more diversity in newsrooms. The homogeneity within newsrooms often fails to represent the diversity of the population they serve accurately. A lack of diverse voices and perspectives hinders the ability to provide nuanced coverage of racial issues and perpetuates biased narratives. Second, the United States still struggles with economic constraints. Media outlets face financial pressures that often compromise their ability to address racial discrimination comprehensively. At times, promoting more diverse content becomes a secondary priority due to commercial considerations, limiting the dissemination of alternative narratives. Third, media organizations often respond to consumer demand for sensational stories, leading to the perpetuation of racial stereotypes and discriminatory narratives. The need for higher ratings and increased viewership reinforces discriminatory content due to its perceived profitability.

In sum, media racial discrimination has significant implications for social harmony and equality. Through reinforcing stereotypes, sustaining systemic inequalities, and promoting bias, media plays a crucial role in perpetuating racial discrimination. However, by addressing the lack of representation, prioritizing diversity, and promoting ethical practices, media organizations can redefine cultural narratives and contribute to a more inclusive and equitable society. Fostering collaboration, supporting media literacy initiatives, and taking collective action will be pivotal in challenging racial discrimination in media and elevating diverse voices in public discourse.

Level 5: Cultural Racial Discrimination

Cultural racial discrimination is a profoundly complex issue that has plagued societies throughout history. Stemming from deep-rooted prejudices, power dynamics, and historical legacies, this form of discrimination has harmed individuals and communities worldwide. We will explore the dimensions, causes, and consequences of cultural racial discrimination, acknowledging its significance in the context of higher education and highlighting the importance of combating it to attain equality.

Cultural racial discrimination manifests itself in various dimensions, ranging from overt acts of hatred to more subtle, institutionalized forms, all contributing to the perpetuation of inequality and discrimination. One manifestation is the imposition of cultural norms and values as the standard by which all other cultures are judged. This leads to the marginalization and exclusion of individuals from different cultural backgrounds who do not conform to these norms. For instance, Western cultural dominance has often resulted in the dismissal or disregard of non-Western cultural practices, viewing them as inferior, outside, or "exotic." Cultural racial discrimination extends beyond personal bias and systemic barriers to root itself into social climate and atmosphere.

The impact of cultural racism is pervasive and deeply felt by individuals and communities on multiple levels. First, it perpetuates systemic barriers that hinder access to equal opportunities, such as education, employment, and healthcare. The devaluation of cultures and identities outside the dominant paradigm restricts social mobility and reinforces the cycle of poverty and marginalization experienced by many racialized communities.

Furthermore, cultural racism perpetuates harmful stereotypes and biases, leading to social exclusion, microaggressions, and racial profiling. The psychological toll of experiencing constant racism and discrimination can result in decreased self-esteem, increased stress levels, and compromised mental health for those targeted by cultural racism.

In addition, cultural racism undermines social cohesion and perpetuates divisions within societies. By excluding and marginalizing certain cultural groups, it fosters a climate of resentment, anger, and distrust, hindering the ability of communities to come together and work toward shared goals.

Whiteness Concepts. Whiteness scholarship has identified a range of concepts. To date, there are five ideological indicators of Whiteness. *Colorblind racial attitude* refers to the belief that race is irrelevant in contemporary society (Neville et al., 2000). *White Ignorance* refers to the systematic obliviousness of Whites concerning racial and ethnic inequality (Forman & Lewis, 2006). *White Resistance* occurs when Whites refuse to concede the existence of structural racism (Ringrose, 2007). *White Innocence* occurs when Whites refuse to acknowledge how they contribute to the racist structures of society (Ross, 1990). Finally, *Racial apathy* denotes indifference and unresponsiveness to racial inequality and related social justice measures (Forman & Lewis, 2015).

To understand the complexities of racial discrimination at the cultural level, it is crucial to explore the concept of Whiteness and its role in perpetuating a system that privileges individuals based on their race. Whiteness originated in the colonial era when European powers embarked on a mission to colonize and dominate various parts of the world. As these nations sought to legitimize their domination, they constructed a narrative that portrayed Whiteness as superior and other races, particularly people of color, as inferior. This system of racial categorization enabled colonizers to assert control over resources, labor, and power, leading to enduring racial hierarchies.

Racializing others is central to the concept of Whiteness. By designating certain groups as "different" and implying inherently inferior, Whiteness reinforces racial discrimination by creating a binary distinction between dominant and subordinate races. Individuals who possess white skin privilege benefit from the systemic advantages that come with their racial identity, while non-White or BIPOC individuals are subjected to societal marginalization and discrimination.

While Whiteness tends to be positioned as the normative racial identity, the concept of intersectionality recognizes that race intersects with other forms of discrimination, including gender, sexuality, and socioeconomic status. For individuals who embody multiple marginalized identities, the interconnected nature of different forms of discrimination exacerbates their experiences of racial discrimination, making it crucial to address the intersecting nature of oppression. Although this book focuses on racism and racial discrimination, it still recognizes the negative consequences of other forms of discrimination, including gender, sexuality, socioeconomic status, and various forms of "isms" (e.g., sexism).

White Fragility. White fragility plays a critical role in perpetuating racial discrimination. First, it stifles conversations about race, making it challenging to address and dismantle systemic racism. When individuals who benefit from White privilege become defensive or avoidant in discussions about racism, progress toward equality is hindered. White fragility silences the voices of marginalized communities, distorting the narrative and perpetuating a status quo that favors White individuals.

Second, White fragility reinforces the impact of racial microaggressions. Microaggressions, subtle and often unconscious acts of racism, perpetuate racial discrimination by maintaining power imbalances and dehumanizing people of color. White fragility usually manifests when White individuals feel accused of these acts, leading to resistance and further marginalization of those affected. The inability to acknowledge microaggressions and their consequences sustains a hostile environment for people of color, hindering their well-being and progression.

Furthermore, White fragility serves as a psychological defense to maintain the White individual's self-image as a "good person" despite benefiting from systemic racism. This defense mechanism avoids confronting the uncomfortable reality of racial inequality and absolves individuals of any responsibility or accountability for perpetuating racial discrimination. This negates the possibility of collective action and prevents systemic change from occurring.

Scientific racism. Scientific racism, a factor contributing to cultural racial discrimination, is a term referring to the pseudoscientific justification of racial hierarchies and inequality and has had a long and contentious history. Scientific racism played a crucial role in justifying colonial expansion and the subjugation of indigenous populations. The belief that racial categories are valid justifies the inferiority of people from different races/ethnicities to White people. Scientific racism, also known as race biology or racial hygiene, refers to the use of supposedly scientific techniques and research to justify racial hierarchies and perpetuate discriminatory practices.

Although it damages both BIPOC and White people, scientific racism has a long history, and it emerged during the nineteenth and early twentieth centuries. Although widely discredited today, its repercussions continue to shape society. It is critical to explore the reasons why scientific racism negatively impacts diverse communities, highlighting its historical contexts and contemporary implications.

RACIAL INCLUSION

Racial inclusion is a multifaceted concept that promotes the equitable participation, recognition, and empowerment of individuals from all racial and ethnic backgrounds within various societal sectors. It emphasizes the creation of an environment where diverse racial identities are acknowledged and valued, allowing for the full expression and development of each individual's potential. Particularly relevant to scholars, psychologists, counselors, and graduate students, racial inclusion involves acknowledging the existence of racial and cultural differences and actively working to dismantle barriers and systems of oppression that perpetuate racial inequities. This consists of implementing inclusive policies, practices, and curricula that respect and integrate many racial experiences and perspectives. Through such proactive measures, racial inclusion seeks to foster a society where everyone, regardless of their racial background, has equal access to opportunities, resources, and the chance to contribute meaningfully to their communities and fields of study. In book writing, this definition can serve as a foundational principle that underlines the importance of designing inclusive narratives, research, and therapeutic practices that reflect the nuanced realities of racially diverse populations.

The concept of racial inclusion encompasses the fundamental idea that all individuals, regardless of their race or ethnicity, should have equal access and opportunities in all elements of society. Achieving racial inclusion requires dismantling systems of discrimination and bias that perpetuate racial inequalities. It entails creating a society where individuals from diverse racial backgrounds are embraced, treated fairly, and have their voices heard. Emphasizing education as a critical facilitator of racial inclusion, it is essential that education and training be integrated into all levels of racial inclusion.

Foundations of Racial Inclusion

Racial inclusion will come true with the collaboration among people across different races/ethnicities. Recognizing culture-related strengths through racial inclusion significantly strengthens social cohesion. When people feel acknowledged and appreciated for their cultural heritage, they are more likely to participate and contribute to society actively. This sense of belonging fosters social integration and equitable opportunities for all. Racially inclusive societies enjoy increased civic engagement, reduced social inequalities, and improved overall collective well-being. By recognizing culture-related strengths, societies can build bridges between different racial groups, avoid exclusion, discrimination, and marginalization, and promote a united front against divisive attitudes.

Below are four principles of the foundation for racial inclusion: (a) empathy and openness toward racial inclusion, (b) recognizing culture-related strengths, (c) challenging stereotypes and promoting understanding, (d) fostering tolerance and unity, and (e) creating safe spaces.

Empathy and Openness Toward Racial Inclusion

In a rapidly globalizing world, where individuals from diverse racial and ethnic backgrounds interact more frequently than ever, fostering empathy and openness toward racial inclusion is crucial. Empathy, defined as the ability to understand and share the feelings of another, and openness, characterized by a willingness to engage with and learn from different racial groups, are essential qualities for building harmonious coexistence and promoting social progress. This book aims to explore the importance of empathy and openness toward racial inclusion and how they can be cultivated through education and policy implementation.

Cross-cultural empathy serves as a bridge that connects individuals from different racial backgrounds, allowing them to recognize and validate each other's experiences. Cross-cultural empathy is appreciating and considering the differences and similarities of another culture compared to one's own. People with cultural empathy are more tolerant of the differences of other cultures. By demonstrating empathy, individuals can gain a deeper understanding of the challenges and triumphs faced by their racial counterparts. This understanding is vital for dismantling prejudice and promoting equal opportunities for all. Research has proven that empathy can help reduce racial bias, increase feelings of connectedness, and enhance affirmative attitudes toward racial inclusion (Trobst et al., 2020). In an educational context, cultivating empathy among students can foster a sense of empathy and solidarity, allowing them to see beyond themselves and embrace the perspectives and experiences of others.

Openness toward racial inclusion entails a genuine willingness to engage with and learn from different racial groups. Openness to racial inclusion also means that individuals demonstrate curiosity toward diversity. It involves recognizing and valuing the contributions and perspectives of individuals from diverse backgrounds. Openness enables individuals to challenge preconceived notions and biases, fostering acceptance and appreciation for racial diversity. Society benefits significantly from transparency, enriching cultural exchange, increasing creativity, and enhancing problem-solving abilities. For instance, research has shown that teams comprising individuals from diverse racial backgrounds are more innovative and effective due to the different knowledge and perspectives they bring to the table (Gupta et al., 2018). Therefore, promoting openness toward racial inclusion is morally right and provides tangible benefits to society.

Recognize Culture-related Strengths

Cultural diversity is a valuable resource that should be cherished and celebrated. Each culture has its unique traditions, history, and values. By recognizing and embracing these diverse perspectives, societies can leverage the strengths of different cultures to create a better world. One culture may excel in the creative arts, while another may possess exceptional scientific knowledge. Recognizing these culture-related strengths allows for collaboration and innovation, enhancing the overall cultural richness of society. By appreciating and respecting cultural diversity, racial inclusion becomes an essential component in harnessing these strengths. For example, Asian culture emphasizes relational harmony and the collective good over individual interests. This cultural trait allows for greater acceptance of change that benefits the entire organization or community. Such a focus on harmony may promote connections and engagement among people from different racial backgrounds.

Another example is Black people's enthusiastic and positive attitude toward diversity. Such passion and enthusiasm toward new happenings will inspire BIPOC and White people to embrace diversity. Likewise, White people also have their culture-related strengths to contribute to the United States.

Challenging Stereotypes and Promoting Understanding

Stereotypes often emerge from a need for more knowledge and experience between different cultures. Racial inclusion necessitates education and awareness to overcome these biases and misconceptions. By actively recognizing and challenging stereotypes, individuals can gain a deeper understanding of various cultures, paving the way for mutual respect and appreciation. Learning about other cultures allows people to recognize different racial groups' talents, traditions, and values, breaking down barriers and fostering inclusivity.

Fostering Tolerance and Unity

Racial inclusion plays a pivotal role in promoting greater tolerance and harmony. By recognizing culture-related strengths, individuals can appreciate the talents and contributions of people from different racial backgrounds. This recognition acts as a unifying force, creating a sense of belonging and acceptance for all individuals, regardless of race or cultural background. Such inclusivity promotes a harmonious coexistence where people feel valued, understood, and celebrated for their unique contributions.

Creating Safe Spaces

Creating safe spaces for open dialogue and discussion is another crucial element in fostering racial inclusion. It is essential to establish an environment where individuals from different racial backgrounds feel comfortable expressing themselves and engaging in conversations about race and racism. This can be achieved through education programs, community initiatives, and the media by promoting diverse perspectives and narratives. By encouraging empathy, understanding, and mutual respect, societies can foster a culture that actively incorporates racial diversity.

Levels of Racial Inclusion

Racial discrimination has five levels, from individual racial discrimination to cultural racial discrimination. Racial inclusion will be stronger and more powerful by addressing it at five levels: (a) individual racial inclusion, (b) institutional racial inclusion, (c) social racial inclusion, (d) media racial inclusion, and (e) cultural racial inclusion.

Level 1: Individual Racial Inclusion

Individual racism perpetuates a cycle of inequality and marginalization, hindering social cohesion and harmony within society. It creates divisions and fosters an "us vs. them" mentality, undermining collective progress and fostering social tension. To promote racial inclusion, individuals can learn to apply acceptance and appreciation to understand people from diverse backgrounds.

Level 2: Institutional Racial Inclusion

Criminal Justice System. To increase racial inclusion in the criminal justice system, it is critical to revise it to restore equity and fairness in the system and increase public trust in the legal system. Communities impacted by racial disparities often perceive the system as unjust, leading to distrust, alienation, and diminished cooperation with law enforcement. Such sentiments hinder effective crime prevention, investigation, and community policing efforts. Consequently, rebuilding trust by dismantling existing racial disparities and actively engaging marginalized communities becomes paramount.

Inclusive reforms that consider community voices, such as participatory budgeting, community-led policing, and restorative justice measures, can help bridge the gap between law enforcement agencies and communities. By involving residents in the decision-making processes and focusing on community-based solutions, the criminal justice system can gain credibility and legitimacy.

Education. Despite the importance of racial inclusion in education, various challenges continue to hinder its realization. One key challenge is the persistent racial achievement gap, where students from specific racial backgrounds consistently underperform compared to their peers. This gap can be attributed to systemic biases and structural barriers that limit access to quality education for marginalized racial groups. Additionally, stereotypes and implicit biases among educators can perpetuate disparities in discipline and academic opportunities for students of color.

Moreover, racially homogeneous teaching staff and curricula lacking diversity contribute to the challenges of promoting racial inclusion in education.

When students do not see themselves represented within the teaching staff or in the curriculum, they may feel marginalized or that their experiences are not valued. This lack of representation reinforces the notion that certain races deserve fewer educational opportunities.

Strategies for Promoting Racial Inclusion in Education. The goal of achieving racial inclusion in education requires a multifaceted approach involving various stakeholders. To begin, policymakers must address the systemic barriers and inequities that perpetuate racial disparities in educational access, resources, and opportunities. This includes equitable funding, diversifying the teaching workforce, implementing culturally responsive pedagogy, and providing comprehensive support systems for students from marginalized racial backgrounds. Integrating inclusive and multicultural curricula in schools and universities helps challenge prejudice, dispel stereotypes, and foster empathy. Increased public awareness campaigns can also facilitate greater understanding and support for policies addressing racial discrimination.

Furthermore, creating inclusive curricula that accurately represent the histories, cultures, and contributions of diverse racial groups is imperative. Providing students with diverse perspectives in their educational materials can foster empathy, understanding, and appreciation for different races and ethnicities. Educators must also engage in ongoing diversity training to recognize and address implicit biases that may affect their instructional practices and student interactions.

Lastly, fostering a sense of belonging and community within educational institutions can contribute to racial inclusion. Schools and universities should create safe spaces that celebrate diversity, engage in open dialogue on racial issues, and actively promote inclusivity. Facilitating opportunities for racial integration, such as extracurricular programs and events that encourage cross-cultural interactions, can also be effective in fostering racial harmony among students.

Level 3: Social Racial Inclusion

To promote racial inclusion at the social level, it is important to fulfill the strategies below: (a) dismantling systems of inequality, (b) challenging the Current Public Policy and Legislation, and (c) community engagement and government support.

Dismantling Systems of Inequality. Racial inclusion is contingent upon dismantling systems of inequality and rectifying historical injustices. Addressing systemic racism requires acknowledging the ways in which institutions perpetuate racial disparities. Education, for example, plays a critical role in fostering racial inclusion. By ensuring equitable access to quality education, regardless of racial background, societies can equip individuals with the tools necessary to thrive. Moreover, inclusive hiring practices, promotion policies, and diversity training in the workplace are essential in eradicating racial discrimination, fostering a culture of equity, and creating opportunities for underrepresented racial groups.

Challenge the Current Public Policy and Legislation. Another foundational factor in establishing racial inclusion is developing and implementing inclusive public policies and legislation. Thus, it is critical to challenge the current public policy and legislation to reduce disparities and promote the equality of public policies. Governments have a role to play in crafting laws that safeguard racial equality and provide resources to uplift marginalized communities. Affirmative action policies, for example, aim to address past injustices by favoring underrepresented groups in areas such as education and employment. However, it is crucial to strike a balance between providing opportunities and maintaining meritocracy, ensuring that all individuals have equal access to opportunities while acknowledging individual capacities and qualifications. Enhancing legal protections against racial discrimination, such as stricter enforcement measures, providing legal aid, and expanding the scope of protection, will enable victims to seek justice more effectively.

Community Engagement and Government Support. Working collaboratively with marginalized communities and involving them in policymaking processes can ensure that policies cater to their needs. Community-led initiatives can empower individuals, fostering long-term inclusion and equality. Apart from educational efforts, governments and institutions should actively implement policies that promote empathy and openness toward racial inclusion. This can be achieved through legislative measures that safeguard equal rights and opportunities for all racial groups. Policies should address systemic inequalities, challenge racial stereotypes, and promote diversity and inclusion within workplaces, public institutions, and community spaces. Initiatives like affirmative action, diversity quotas, and anti-discrimination laws are examples of policy measures that can effectively advance racial inclusion (Pager et al., 2009). Public awareness campaigns can also be launched to raise awareness about racial biases and foster empathy among the general public.

Level 4: Media Racial Inclusion

In the media level of racial inclusion, it is necessary to apply the four strategies below:

Increased Diversity and Representation. Media organizations should actively work toward diversifying their staff, including journalists, writers, editors, and executives. A diverse workforce will bring varied perspectives and insights that can challenge existing biases and improve representation.

Ethical Guidelines and Sensitivity Training. Media outlets should develop and enforce clear ethical guidelines in reporting, ensuring balanced representation and fair portrayals of racial minorities. Mandatory training and education programs on cultural sensitivity can sensitize media professionals to the impact of their work on marginalized communities.

Collaborative Partnerships and Accountability. Collaboration between media organizations, minority communities, and civil rights organizations can foster a collective effort to address racial discrimination in media. Establishing accountability mechanisms, such as public feedback channels or diversity audits, can increase transparency and encourage corrective actions.

Media Literacy. Promoting media literacy is crucial to enabling consumers to navigate media content critically. Educational institutions and community organizations should incorporate media literacy programs that teach individuals how to identify and challenge racial discrimination perpetuated by media narratives.

Level 5: Cultural Racial Inclusion

In order to combat racial discrimination effectively, it is imperative to address White fragility. First and foremost, education and awareness are critical. Recognizing the manifestation of White fragility and understanding its implications are essential for White individuals to begin dismantling their biases and challenging their privilege. Anti-racist education should be integrated into curricula at all levels, promoting honest conversations and creating safe spaces for discussions about race.

Fostering empathy and building relationships across racial lines can help alleviate White fragility. Genuine conversations that center on the experiences and concerns of people of color can assist in breaking down stereotypes, humanizing marginalized communities, and enabling a deeper understanding of racial inequalities. By listening and learning from diverse perspectives, White individuals become better equipped to acknowledge their own biases and actively work toward dismantling discriminatory systems.

White fragility serves as a significant barrier to addressing and dismantling racial discrimination. By understanding how it perpetuates systemic racism, society can work toward collectively combating these inherent biases. By challenging White fragility through education, awareness, and open dialogue, individuals can actively contribute to creating a more equitable world. Ultimately, White fragility must be confronted head-on to form a society that not only rejects racial discrimination but also actively promotes justice, equality, and inclusivity for all.

Chapter 1

Racial Discrimination

Costs and Consequences

In the fight against racism, neither BIPOC nor Whites are winners. While BIPOC experience racial traumas or trauma-related symptoms, White people suffer from racial discrimination and struggle with White fragility and emotional distress such as White guilt. This chapter explores in-depth the costs and consequences of racial discrimination against BIPOC and White people in the United States. Because racial discrimination based on group-related characters is a violation of human rights and "Federal laws prohibit discrimination based on a person's national origin, race, color, religion, sex, and familial status. Laws prohibiting national origin discrimination make it illegal to discriminate because of a person's birthplace, ancestry, culture, or language" (Department of Justice, 2000). To date, unfortunately, racial discrimination is still prevalent in our daily lives, from interpersonal interaction to policymaking. Such prevalence of racial discrimination presents two significant consequences: (a) consequences of racial discrimination to BIPOC and (b) damages and costs of racial discrimination to White people.

CONSEQUENCES OF RACIAL DISCRIMINATION TO BIPOC

Racial discrimination is a traumatic experience that haunts BIPOC individuals throughout their lives. It does not occur randomly, unexpectedly, or unpredictably, affecting them in various ways. Conversely, because racial discrimination includes many levels of racism (see introduction), racial discrimination also operates systematically and structurally, encompassing multiple levels of racism that damage the well-being of BIPOC communities.

For example, individual racism has profound impacts on its victims, resulting in psychological, emotional, and even physical harm. Individuals who experience racism may suffer from a diminished sense of self-worth, increased stress, anxiety, depression, and a heightened sense of vulnerability. The cumulative effect of constant discrimination can lead to long-lasting damage to an individual's mental well-being. Moreover, individual racism perpetuates a cycle of inequality and marginalization, hindering social cohesion and harmony within society. It creates divisions and an "us vs. them" mentality, undermining collective progress and fostering social tension.

Generic Stress Model

By developing an 18-item self-report inventory of the Schedule of Racist Events (SRE), Landrine and Klonoff (1996) found the high frequency and severe intensity of racist events that happened to Black people. Their findings of the high frequency and vigorous intensity of racist events experienced by Black people echo the argument that racial discrimination exists in and includes various levels of racism. Landrine and Klonoff (1996) applied generic stress theory and studies by Lazarus (1996) and other scholars (Billings & Moos, 1981) to capture the racist events experienced by Black people. They also conceptualized racist events as adverse events or stressors that happen to "*African Americans because they are African Americans*" (Landrine & Klonoff, 1996, p. 146). However, no one should be destined to endure racist experiences, regardless of their racial background. Black people and other BIPOC face the burden of racial trauma not due to their racial and ethnic origins but as a result of the prevailing institutional racism they encounter.

As a pioneering scale in the racism-related scale, Landrine and Klonoff's (1996) SRE adopted two approaches to assessing stress to measure Black people's experiences with stress. One approach is the frequency of the racist events that Black people experience as stressful. The other approach is Black people's appraisal or evaluation of the racist events as stressful. The SRE includes eighteen items, such as "How many times have you been mistreated by *teachers and professors* because you are Black?," "How many times have you been mistreated by your *employers, bosses and supervisors* because you are Black?," and "How many times have you been treated unfairly by *people in service jobs* (store clerks, waiters, bartenders, bank tellers, and others) because you are Black?" Under each item, participants answer the frequency "How many times in the past year?" and "How many times in your entire life?". Participants also answer intensity questions such as "How stressful was this for you?"

The combination of frequency and intensity of racial stress in Black people's cultural context led Landrine and Klonoff (1996) to develop an exemplary scale to assess racism-related stress (SRE). This scale (SRE) was used to measure racism-related stress across different races (Lang, 2001), including Portuguese (Zubaran et al., 2020) and African American women (DeBlaere & Moradi, 2008). Notably et al. (1996) SRE was cited in 715 publications in the PsycInfo database. The extremely high volume of citations of the SRE indicates five key points regarding racism-related stress studies.

First, it shows the increasing awareness of the persistent issue of racism-related stress and its adverse impacts on BIPOCs and their communities. More importantly, researchers and scholars on racism and racism-related stress begin to apply scientific frameworks to conceptualize the detrimental effects of racism-related stress on BIPOCs. With meticulous methodology and rigorous analyses, scholars provide strong and persuasive evidence to demonstrate how racism-related stress damages the physical and mental health of BIPOCs.

Second, the pioneer scholars' racism-related stress studies are pivotal as they bring people's attention to the physical and psychological problems related to racism. That being said, the improvement of the physical and mental health of BIPOCs begins with scientific research on racism-related stress.

Third, the studies on racism-related stress strengthen and promote clinicians' evidence-based practice. As the foundation of training in APA's scientist-practitioner model (Baker & Benjamin, 2000), science without practice would be abstract, and practice without science would be blind. To integrate scientific research and clinical practice on racism-related stress, it is inevitable to train and prepare psychologists to be able to provide services and conduct research on mental health problems such as racism-related stress. The purpose of the APA's scientist-practitioner model is to ensure that practitioners can integrate scientific knowledge with clinical practice to enhance their best practice with clients. Contextualizing APA's model in clients' cultural backgrounds requires practitioners' integration of their critical thinking and multicultural sensitivity to address clients' trauma or stress related to their racism.

Fourth, because Landrine and Klonoff's (1996) SRE addressed racism in the workplace, contextualizing racism-related stress in BIPOC's workplace will provide people with a comprehensive picture that BIPOC tolerate stress in their work environment. Racism in institutional discrimination can have profound effects on the professional growth and well-being of minority employees. A hostile work environment, characterized by bias, exclusion, and limited opportunities, can lead to increased stress, decreased job satisfaction, and lower levels of commitment to the organization. Research has shown that individuals experiencing workplace discrimination are more likely to suffer from mental health issues, including anxiety and depression. The mental toll of discrimination can result in decreased productivity, higher absenteeism rates, and increased turnover among minority employees. These negative impacts on well-being and professional growth can perpetuate cycles of inequality, leaving minorities at a disadvantage in terms of career opportunities and advancement.

Fifth, since Landrine and Klonoff's (1996) pioneering scale of SRE, after the 1980s and 1990s, there have been more studies on racism-related stress. The prolific focus on multicultural research, especially racism, in turn, results in promoting the awareness of social justice. One mission of the racism-related stress research is to expose and report the damages and adverse effects of racism on BIPOC and advocate for systemic and institutional change. Thus, scientific research on racism-related stress will make the advocacy more substantial and more persuasive to empower institutional and systemic change.

Biopsychosocial Model

A few years later, after Landrine and Klonoff's (1996) SRE, Clark et al. (1999) also addressed Black people's experiences of racism and stress. Different from Landrine and Klonoff's (1996) model, Clark et al. (1999) address racism as a stressor for Black people with a biopsychosocial model. Before Clark et al., there were few studies examining the effects of racism within the framework of a comprehensive biopsychosocial model. Different from the generic stress model in Landrine and Klonoff's (1996) SRE, which measures Black people's frequency and intensity of racism-related stress, Clark et al. (1999) have integrated Black people's perception of an environmental stimulus as racist, resulting in amplified psychological and physiological stress responses. These responses are influenced by various factors, including constitutional, sociodemographic, psychological, behavioral, and coping responses.

Clark et al.'s (1999) article raised four points in the research and clinical practice of multicultural counseling. First, racism-related stress in Clark et al.'s article shifted and expanded the focus of racism to Black people's chronological experience. Racism was conceptualized in the context of racial discrimination, institutional discrimination, and microaggression. Racism is a chronic stressor for Black people who live in an environment filled with racism for almost their lifetime. Such chronic racism-related stress highlights that Black people are exposed to racism from their birth and throughout their development. Because Black people are exposed to racism in interpersonal interactions, school, workplace, and society, the racial discrimination, microaggressions, and institutional racism they experience can lead to their psychological distress, trauma, and compromised physical health.

Second, Clark et al.'s article addressed that racism-related stress is detrimental to Black people's physical health *and* psychological well-being. Such breakthrough findings inspire future research to comprehensively investigate the negative impacts of racism on Black people regarding their physical health, such as heart disease and diabetes, in addition to psychological distress. These physical health problems also reveal disparities in healthcare facilities, hospitals, access to fresh produce, and fitness centers between Black and White neighborhoods (Gaskin et al., 2012).

Third, Clark et al.'s (1999) article promotes health disparities research because their article demonstrates the clear connection between racism, social environment, and the damages of racism to physical health and psychological well-being. Health disparities refer to the unequal and unfair distribution of healthcare and health outcomes among people across races/ethnicities. Despite significant advancements in medicine and public health in the twenty-first century, disparities persist and pose a challenge to achieving health equity among different populations, especially between BIPOC and the majority of Whites. Clark et al.'s article, with a biopsychosocial model, sets up a new direction to connect racism to health disparities. While understanding the causes, contributing factors, and consequences of health disparities is critical to reducing these disparities, it is equally important to know the causes and consequences of racism to minimize its impacts.

Fourth, Clark et al.'s (1999) article addresses the issue of racism within academic settings. It highlights the underrepresentation of Black people and BIPOC individuals in higher education. For instance, data from the National Center for Education Statistics reveal that Black faculty make up only about 6 percent of all faculty members in colleges and universities, despite Black people comprising 13 percent of the total national population. Furthermore, the number of Black faculty decreases significantly as one moves up the ranks of academia (Conner, 2022).

Race-based Traumatic Stress

Carter (2007) commented on racism research by scholars (e.g., Clark et al., 1999; Landrine & Klonoff, 1996) that "they have not considered whether racism may produce trauma" (15), and then he conceptualized "the possible role of racism as trauma in . . . people of Color" (37). According to the DSM-5 (American Psychiatric Association, 2013, p. 271), the first four criteria for post-traumatic stress disorder (PTSD) are:

A. Exposure to actual or threatened death, serious injury, or sexual violence in one (or more) of the following ways: directly experiencing the traumatic event(s) or witnessing, in person, the event(s) as it occurred to others.

B. Presence of one (or more) of the following intrusion symptoms associated with the traumatic event(s), beginning after the traumatic event(s) occurred:
C. Recurrent, involuntary, and intrusive distressing memories of the traumatic event(s).
D. Dissociative reactions (e.g., flashbacks) in which the individual feels or acts as if the traumatic event(s) were recurring. (Such reactions may occur on a continuum, with the most extreme expression being a complete loss of awareness of present surroundings.)
E. Persistent avoidance of stimuli associated with the traumatic event(s), beginning after the traumatic event(s) occurred, as evidenced by one or both of the following:
F. Avoidance of or efforts to avoid distressing memories, thoughts, or feelings about or closely associated with the traumatic event(s).
G. Avoidance of or efforts to avoid external reminders (people, places, conversations, activities, objects, situations) that arouse distressing memories, thoughts, or feelings about or closely associated with the traumatic event(s).
H. Negative alterations in cognitions and mood associated with the traumatic event(s), beginning or worsening after the traumatic event(s) occurred, as evidenced by two (or more) of the following:
   a. Inability to remember an essential aspect of the traumatic event(s) (typically due to dissociative amnesia, and not to other factors such as head injury, alcohol, or drugs).
   b. Persistent and exaggerated negative beliefs or expectations about oneself, others, or the world (e.g., "I am bad," "No one can be trusted," "The world is perilous," "My whole nervous system is permanently ruined").
   c. Persistent, distorted cognitions about the cause or consequences of the traumatic event(s) that lead the individual to blame himself/herself or others.
   d. Persistent negative emotional state (e.g., fear, horror, anger, guilt, or shame).

According to DSM-5, the rest of the four criteria include:

> (1) marked alterations in arousal and reactivity associated with the traumatic event(s), the duration of the disturbance (Criteria B, C, D, and E) is more than 1 month, the disturbance causes clinically significant distress or impairment in social, occupational, or other important areas of functioning, and the disturbance is not attributable to the physiological effects of a substance (e.g., medication, alcohol) or another medical condition. (American Psychiatric Association, 2013, p. 272)

Based on the above DSM-5 criteria, it is clear that BIPOC individuals suffer various levels of racial discrimination (e.g., individual racism and institutional racism) in numerous contexts (e.g., shopping and the criminal justice system). Thus, BIPOC individuals live in an environment with traumatic experiences, which may trigger PTSD symptoms.

While Landrine and Klonoff (1996) measured racist events using a generic stress model, Clark et al. (1999) tested racism as a stressor within a biopsychosocial model. Carter's (2007) article, "Racism and Psychological and Emotional Injury: Recognizing and Assessing Race-Based Traumatic Stress," conceptualizes racism as a traumatic event. Subsequently, Carter et al. (2013) developed the Race-Based Traumatic Stress Symptom Scale (RBTS) to assess racially traumatic events and their impact on BIPOC individuals. Carter (2007) and his colleagues (2013) also highlight that traumatic race-related events can range from personal experiences or interpersonal interactions involving racial discrimination and microaggressions to racial violence and tragedies. The connection between racism and PTSD reactions aligns with the book's definitions of racial discrimination in the Introduction, which encompass various levels of racism, from individual to policy level. According to Carter et al. (2013), the effects of RBTS can be both immediate and long-lasting, leading to significant psychological distress and negatively affecting an individual's well-being. RBTS can also be triggered months or even years after the experience of racism-related stress among BIPOC individuals. These triggers can stem from a single traumatic event or multiple cumulative traumatic experiences (Pieterse et al., 2024).

Carter et al.'s (2013) RBTSS attempts to provide a comprehensive assessment of the BIPOC's psychological and emotional impact of experiences related to racial discrimination and violence. It includes items about (a) psychological symptoms, such as emotional and cognitive responses to racial trauma; (b) behavioral symptoms, such as behavioral responses to racial trauma; (c) physiological symptoms, such as headaches; and (d) sociopolitical factors, such as systemic racism.

In sum, the RBTSS assesses racism and its traumatic impact on BIPOC's psychological, behavioral, and physiological responses. It appears more comprehensive than previous models and scales on racism-related stress. Importantly, RBTSS aligns its scale items with the criteria in DSM-5 (Ng & Chu, 2024).

Carter's (2007) theoretical model and Carter et al.'s (2013) RBTSS significantly contribute to the research and clinical practice regarding racism-related stress. First, the RBTSS clearly recognizes the awareness of the severe and intense impact of racial trauma related to racism. The RBTSS is one of the scales conceptualizing racism as a traumatic experience for BIPOC (Ng & Chu, 2024; Pieterse et al., 2024). By aligning the mental health consequences with racial trauma, the RBTSS, in turn, opens a door to include racism-related stress in trauma-informed therapy in a multicultural sensitive approach. Second, because of the comprehensiveness of the RBTSS, there is more attention from scholars and practitioners to applying evidence-based practices to racism-related stress (Alvarez et al., 2022). Third, the RBTSS promotes culturally appropriate and sensitive psychotherapy by cultivating an understanding of racial trauma and the consequences experienced by BIPOC.

A Model of Integration of Racial Trauma and BIPOC's Strength

Chao (in progress) developed a racial trauma scale that includes items about racism-related stress and the resilience and strengths of racial minority populations. According to Comas-Díaz et al. (2019), "Racial trauma, or race-based stress, refers to the events of danger related to real or perceived experience of racial discrimination" (p. 1). The definition of racial trauma focuses on real or the perception of racism-related stress. Moreover, in addition to respecting the real perception of racial trauma, Comas-Díaz et al. (2019) highlight historical trauma, stating that "severe psychological and physiological trauma can have intergenerational effects. Similarly, historical trauma or soul wounds—the cumulative psychological wounds resulting from historical traumatic experiences" (2). (Please see the introduction of this book for more details about historical trauma.) Besides discussing historical trauma, Comas-Díaz et al. (2019) also explore resilience as coping strategies when BIPOC encounter racial trauma.

Different from the generic stress model (Landrine & Klonoff, 1996), the biopsychosocial model (Clark et al., 1999), and race-based traumatic stress (Carter et al., 2013) on racism-related stress, Chao (in process) proposed that racial trauma needs to be integrated with BIPOC's strengths such as resilience. The BIPOC promote social justice and racial trauma healing because they suffer from racism (Comas-Díaz & Jacobsen, 2024). That is, BIPOC may thrive against racism-related stress with their coping strategies and culture-unique strengths (Grier-Reed et al., 2023).

According to Chao (in process), although racial trauma makes a significantly detrimental impact on BIPOC's psychological and physical well-being and health, BIPOC and their communities have been thriving against their racial trauma (Grier-Reed et al., 2023). Specifically, Black people respond to racial trauma with their resilience and post-traumatic growth (Mushonga et al., 2021) in addition to their PTSD symptoms related to racism. The connections between racial trauma and post-traumatic growth indicate two points below. First, to accurately and holistically understand racial trauma (or racism-related stress) and its impacts on BIPOC, it is critical to evaluate the negative consequences and how BIPOC individuals apply their culture-unique strengths to manage or even thrive against racial trauma. Second, while many scholars and clinicians must focus on physical and psychological traumatic reactions from racial trauma, the dominant attention to the negative consequences of racial trauma cannot replace the positive role of BIPOC's strengths in racial trauma. For BIPOC, the culture-related strengths are more than buffers protecting them against trauma; these strengths also serve critical functions in their lives to "deepen connections with others, tap into their inner strengths, gain new perspectives and a new appreciation for life, and connect to spirituality, not only grow but are more likely to report flourishing" (Grier-Reed et al., 2023, p. 41).

Chao (in process)'s "A Model of Integration of Racial Trauma and BIPOC's Strength" aims to provide a comprehensive model that explores the integration of racial trauma and strengths within BIPOC to understand the complexities of racial trauma, trauma healing, and BIPOC flourishing and thriving against racism-related stress.

The role of racial trauma in the model of integration of racial trauma and BIPOC's strength. It is well documented that BIPOC suffer various racial traumas, which causes their physical, psychological, and emotional distress, such as anxiety, depression, PTSD, and lower self-esteem. The racial trauma must be deeply rooted in different levels of racial discrimination, from the individual level to the institutional level, social level, and policy level of racism.

BIPOC Strength. Despite BIPOC suffering different formats and levels of racism, which results in their physical and psychological symptoms, it would miss the comprehensive process of their healing from racial trauma. In the process of racial trauma healing, BIPOC individuals have consistently and persistently demonstrated remarkable strength and resilience. For example, Asian Americans utilize culture-related strengths such as forbearance and perseverance when encountering racial trauma or stressful situations (Wei et al., 2013). Black people may seek spirituality and resilience as resources to manage their racial trauma (Neblett, 2023). Drawing on culture-specific strengths, cultural values and beliefs, spirituality, community resources, and family support, BIPOC individuals and communities transform racial trauma into opportunities to reconnect to their cultural values and strengths. These strengths serve as their protective factors to buffer them from severe damage caused by racial trauma.

DAMAGES AND COSTS OF RACIAL DISCRIMINATION TO WHITE PEOPLE

Racial discrimination hurts just about everyone, not only those BIPOC who suffer racial trauma. The damages and negative consequences impact almost every individual in the United States. Moreover, Metzl (2019) stated that racial anxieties caused White people to make decisions that harmed them. Moreover, racism, racial anger, racial resentment, and racial fear can have detrimental consequences on the well-being of White people (Grzanka et al., 2019; Metzl & MacLeish, 2015).

Racial discrimination is a continuous and pervasive topic that deeply impacts BIPOC communities, and it is often overlooked that the damages and costs of racial discrimination also affect White people. Racial discrimination may significantly harm White people's psychological and emotional well-being. For example, prejudiced and biased attitudes can lead to feelings of White guilt, White shame, and confusion about one's identity (Chao et al., 2015), eventually affecting one's self-esteem and mental health (Metzl, 2019). Racial discrimination also leads to White supremacy and exacerbates feelings of inflexibility, isolation, anxiety, and depression among White individuals (Magnet & Dunnington, 2022).

Although it is dismissed as a marginalized topic, racial discrimination causes various consequences on White people's physical health, psychological well-being, educational and career opportunities, and media portrayal. Racial discrimination also creates numerous unfavorable images against White people. Poussaint (2002) suggests DSM's delusional disorder, prejudice type, to describe extreme racism, and moreover, "Extreme racist delusions can also occur as a major symptom in other psychotic disorders, such as schizophrenia and bipolar disorder. Persons suffering delusions usually have serious social dysfunction that impairs their ability to work with others and maintain employment" (4).

Despite the overwhelming impact of institutional racial discrimination on BIPOC, Metzl (2019) argued that racism ultimately hurts White people's health. While BIPOC individuals suffer significantly from institutional racial discrimination, the health and well-being of White Americans suffer from institutional racial discrimination as well. Reacting to racism-related issues, White people may struggle with psychological harms such as White fragility and emotional distress or reactions (e.g., White guilt, psychosocial costs of racism to Whites [Spanierman & Heppner, 2004], White fatigue, and White vulnerability). Below are detailed descriptions of how racial discrimination damages White people.

White Supremacy

White supremacy is an ideology that asserts the inherent superiority of the White race over other racial or ethnic groups. White supremacy can be defined as the institutionalization of Whiteness and White privilege and the historical, social, political, and economic systems and structures that contribute to its continued dominance and subordination (Giroux & McLaren, 1994).

White supremacy hurts BIPOC's well-being, and they suffer various racial traumas. In fact, White supremacy damages almost everyone's mental health. However, Elliott (2016) listed ten ways in which White supremacy hurts White people, and here are three examples from Elliott's (2016) article.

> Teaching White children from an early age to disconnect from people of color, distance ourselves, understand ourselves as "better than," thereby distorting and putting out of reach real human connection with most of humanity.
>
> [. . .]
>
> Living on this land with no connection or understanding of the land we are on or knowledge of the indigenous peoples it was stolen from. Forcing people of European descent to erase our culture in order to conform to whiteness and white, dominant culture. (Elliott, 2016)

These examples show that White supremacy endorses distance, isolation, and perfectionism. From a psychological perspective, perfectionism and distance sever connections from people. When White people focus on their superiority over people of other races/ethnicities, they are also at risk of losing connections and support from others, which results in deeper isolation.

The consequences of racial discrimination are not limited to individual suffering but also impact White people. These consequences also affect societal dynamics. White people who struggle with racism may harbor feelings of resentment toward BIPOC. Such resentment can increase racial tensions, hinder social progress, and perpetuate a divide that prevents the collaboration necessary for societal advancements.

Whiteness

Efird et al. (2024) conceptualize "Whiteness as the racialized social system and a set of beliefs that uphold White American social supremacy and the oppression of [BIPOC]" (3). Recently, an increasing number of psychologists and scholars have found negative consequences of Whiteness on White people in addition to BIPOC.

It is inevitable to cultivate a deeper understanding of Whiteness and how Whiteness impacts the physical health and psychological and emotional well-being of White people. While White supremacy is related to loneliness and reduced connections to other people, Whiteness also has harmful impacts on White people's mental and health in three ways.

First, Whiteness impacts White people's physical health. While there is increasing awareness of anti-racism among people in the United States, studies are showing that some White people may encounter challenges, stress, and anxiety about being White, or such anxiety may be related to their racial identity (Chao et al., 2015). Such anxiety and feelings of being challenged may result in some White people's increased cortisol levels and subsequent health complications (Bowleg, 2017). Moreover, these concerns signify that Whiteness and its associated cultural ideals can lead to adverse physical health outcomes (Efird & Lightfoot, 2020).

Second, Whiteness can also result in mental health challenges for individuals of White descent. The stress of conforming to societal expectations and the worry of relinquishing racial privileges can substantially affect one's mental well-being. Studies have shown that White individuals who rigidly adhere to cultural norms linked to Whiteness may face intensified feelings of anxiety, depression, and overall psychological distress (Collins & Watson, 2021). It is important to acknowledge that mental health problems impact people regardless of their racial background, debunking common stereotypes. This underscores the harmful effects of Whiteness on emotional well-being.

Third, Whiteness also perpetuates social exclusion among White individuals. By enforcing a system that values homogeneity over diversity, White people often face pressure to conform to perceived norms, thereby stifling their individuality and unique perspectives (Bowleg, 2023). Additionally, the emphasis on maintaining Whiteness as the norm can create a fear of being associated with marginalized groups. Consequently, White people may face social isolation or struggle with building interracial relationships with other people.

White Privileges

White privilege is a societal phenomenon deeply rooted in systemic inequalities across races/ethnicities (Ford et al., 2019). It encompasses the unearned advantages that White individuals experience in various aspects of life, from education and employment to healthcare and criminal justice. While the detrimental effects of racism and discrimination on marginalized groups are widely acknowledged, it is often overlooked that White privilege can damage White people themselves. By examining the psychological, social, and moral implications of White privilege, it becomes evident that its existence perpetuates alienation, disconnection, and an inability to acknowledge and critically address systemic racial inequalities (Efird et al., 2024).

White privilege perpetuates a distorted sense of self-worth and identity dilemmas among White individuals. When individuals repeatedly benefit from unearned advantages solely based on the color of their skin, they are denied the opportunity to develop a genuine sense of accomplishment and self-esteem. Instead, they may feel that their success is partially or wholly attributed to their race, undermining their abilities and achievements. This psychological erosion is detrimental to their overall well-being, hindering personal growth and undermining a healthy sense of self.

Moreover, White privilege fosters ignorance and complacency among White individuals regarding systemic racism. The lack of exposure to the struggles faced by marginalized communities leads to a skewed understanding of the world. Without experiencing firsthand the hardships and discrimination faced by people of color, White individuals may remain oblivious to their participation in perpetuating systemic racism. Thus, their emotional development is limited, impairing their ability to empathize and connect with others deeply. White people may face difficulty in understanding their own identities as they navigate their privilege while being conscious of the social and racial dynamics at play. This struggle to balance the desire to be authentic with privilege awareness can lead to feelings of isolation and social alienation.

Colorblind Racial Attitude

Colorblind racial attitude has gained considerable attention in recent years as a seemingly well-intentioned concept that aims to promote equality and diminish racism. However, colorblind racial attitudes can inadvertently perpetuate racial inequalities and undermine efforts toward achieving true racial harmony (Neville et al., 2000). Colorblind racial attitudes may create detrimental consequences for White people. In the Color-Blind Racial Attitudes Scale (CoBRAS), Neville et al. (2000) described colorblind racial attitude as based on five assumptions: (a) racism exists on structural levels and some White people do not believe themselves part of racism (Hays et al., 2023; Thompson & Neville, 1999); (b) racism creates a system of advantages for White elites only, not for blue-collar White workers (Ford & Sharif, 2020); (c) denial of these realities is the core component of colorblind racial attitudes; (d) people across racial groups can maintain a colorblind perspective; and (e) colorblind racial attitudes are cognitive in nature; they are part of a cognitive schema used to interpret racial stimuli (Neville et al., 2000, p. 61).

However, colorblind racial attitudes harm both BIPOC and White people. Because colorblind attitudes often lead to a denial of White privilege, dismissing the notion that White individuals automatically benefit from historical and societal advantages purely due to their race. The failure to acknowledge White privilege creates barriers to understanding systemic racism and inadvertently perpetuates racial disparities. By refusing to recognize the social, political, and economic advantages that come with being White, potential biases remain unexamined, making it challenging to address and eliminate systemic inequalities in society and academia (King et al., 2023).

Colorblindness obscures the unique experiences and perspectives of marginalized groups, as it puts a blanket of sameness over everyone. Thus, colorblind racial attitudes may contribute to reduced cross-cultural empathy in some White people (French et al., 2020). By failing to recognize the importance of acknowledging and valuing individual racial identities, White people may lose the opportunity for self-awareness and to appreciate the significance of understanding the experiences of others.

Another negative outcome or consequence of colorblind racial attitudes is that they exacerbate implicit microaggressions toward BIPOC. When colorblindness is adopted, White individuals may dismiss or remain unaware of such microaggressions, which perpetuates racial prejudice. Furthermore, failing to recognize these subtle biases can prevent the growth and development of educational environments supporting marginalized students and faculty members. By disregarding the discriminatory implications of microaggressions, White individuals may perpetuate a hostile climate for those who experience them, inhibiting their academic and professional success (Jean et al., 2023).

Negative Emotional Consequences

Racial discrimination not only makes White people self-challenge their racial identity as White individuals, but also causes negative emotional consequences such as White guilt, White fragility, White shame, White fear, White fatigue, and White vulnerability.

White Guilt

White guilt refers to the feelings of guilt experienced by White people due to the historical and contemporary privileges they benefit from at the expense of BIPOC. White guilt may have severe and negative implications for the mental well-being of White people. The burden of guilt can lead to high levels of stress, anxiety, and even depression. Constantly carrying the weight of historical wrongs and the privilege associated with their race can create a sense of self-blame and internal conflict. The pressure to navigate a complex web of identity, morality, and responsibility can be overwhelming for some individuals, leading to a negative impact on their mental health.

Additionally, White guilt may often manifest as a form of moral distress, where individuals feel helpless or paralyzed in their attempts to address societal racial disparities. These feelings of powerlessness can further exacerbate mental health issues and hinder productive action toward social justice. It is crucial to recognize the importance of self-care, seeking therapy, and developing healthier coping mechanisms to address and overcome the negative impact of White guilt.

White guilt may interfere with White people's interpersonal relationships, including relationships within White groups and people of other races/ethnicities. Within the White group, individuals may experience tensions and conflicts with other White peers when there are disagreements in handling White privileges and race-related issues. This guilt may foster self-doubt among White individuals, defensiveness, denial, or resentment, which in turn contributes to a negative impact on White people's well-being and health (Zetzer, 2018).

White guilt may be a barrier for some White people to having a productive dialogue about issues regarding social justice and multicultural issues because White guilt may decrease their self-esteem as White individuals. Such low racial self-esteem may make White people turn to silence or ignore engaging in conversations and developing solutions to handle racism-related issues (Jean et al., 2023).

White Fragility

White fragility is one of the negative psychological consequences that White Americans experience due to racism. Before defining White fragility, it is essential to clarify the differences between White fragility, White privilege, and White supremacy. White privilege refers to the advantages that White people have in society which BIPOC do not have. Additionally, White privilege encompasses the injustice and unequal advantages that White people have over BIPOC. White privilege has been pervasive throughout US history and society. It exists in policies, housing, communities, healthcare, and other invisible systems that have existed and continue to exist in the United States (McIntosh, 2003). White supremacy is the belief that people with White skin are superior to people with non-White skin. Unfortunately, White supremacy is an ideology that promotes the belief that White people are inherently superior to BIPOC. Worse, such a belief system is used to justify discriminatory systems, policies, and decisions in US society (Gorritz, 2024).

Different from White privilege and White supremacy, White fragility refers to the discomfort felt by White people when they are in situations involving discussions around race-related issues such as racial inequality and injustice. For example, a White individual may ask immigrants where they are originally from due to their accent, clothes, or other physical features. The immigrants may want to take this opportunity to talk about implicit racist questions. Such an intention may make White people defensive. White people's defensiveness reflects their hurt feelings. From a psychological perspective, defensive behaviors aim to distract someone from their feelings of being hurt and shame. Likewise, when White people are asked to discuss racism, they may apply defensive mechanisms to protect themselves. Another purpose of the defensive mechanism is to shift the attention and responsibility for the faults to others so that, in turn, White people feel better about themselves (Keramidas, 2021).

The concept of White fragility refers to the fear, anger, and anxiety that arise when White individuals feel challenged or implicated in discussions of race. This defensiveness is rooted in the perceived threat to their identity and can hinder constructive dialogues on racism, obstructing growth and understanding (Williams et al., 2016). Because White fragility refers to the inability or resistance of White individuals to engage in meaningful discussions regarding racial issues, White people may often experience defensiveness, discomfort, and emotional stress when they discuss or engage in conversations or behaviors regarding racial inequality. Coined by DiAngelo (2018), White fragility is deeply entrenched in the institutionalized racism prevalent in modern societies. This fragility arises from the fear of being labeled as racist or realizing personal complicity in perpetuating racial inequalities.

White fragility can cause cognitive dissonance, as individuals struggle to reconcile their self-perception as non-racist with the realities of societal racial imbalances. This dissonance can lead to feelings of guilt, shame, and confusion, negatively impacting mental well-being and overall self-esteem. White fragility may also worsen White fear of being exposed as complicit in racial injustices, which can create anxiety and defensiveness. Acknowledging one's own privilege and unconscious biases can be challenging and uncomfortable, and such discomfort may turn into denial or avoidance (Ford et al., 2022).

White fragility can also result in a threat to White people's development of White racial identity (Paslay, 2020). When confronted with their role in perpetuating racial inequality, White individuals may feel their status quo and social standing are at risk. This fear of losing social capital or facing social exclusion contributes to defensiveness, resistance, and an unwillingness to acknowledge racial privilege or confront systemic racism.

White Shame

White shame refers to an emotional and psychological burden experienced by some White individuals who, upon recognizing historical and contemporary racial inequalities, internalize a sense of guilt, responsibility, or shame. While White shame may appear positive on the surface, as it seemingly encourages introspection and acknowledgment of privilege, it can inadvertently perpetuate a cycle of self-doubt, division, and inaction among White individuals.

In addition to fostering White people's self-doubt, White shame may contribute to some White people's internalized racism and racial stereotypes, leading to a self-blaming of the inherited racism. White people might fear being accused of racism or exhibiting racist behavior at every turn, hampering open dialogue and progress (Spanierman & Heppner, 2004).

Responding to racism-related issues with defensiveness has been some White people's typical reaction (Neville et al., 2000). In an attempt to protect themselves from accusations of racism-related issues, White people may become defensive and distant from engaging in conversations about race. This defensive stance stifles opportunities for education, understanding, and growth. Additionally, it hampers collective efforts toward racial justice, as the focus remains on personal feelings rather than systemic change.

White shame often leads to inaction, as individuals may feel overwhelmed by racial injustices and unsure of how to contribute constructively. The fear of making mistakes or inadvertently perpetuating inequality can immobilize White individuals, leading to a perpetuation of the status quo. In this sense, White shame reinforces a damaging cycle in which individuals remain silent and detached from efforts to dismantle systemic racism (Malat et al., 2018).

White Fear

White fear can have detrimental effects on mental health. Fear is a natural response to perceived threats, but it can have severe consequences when it becomes pervasive and irrational. In the case of White fear, individuals may develop anxiety disorders, depression, or chronic stress. The constant worry about potential harm or loss of privilege can lead to hypervigilance, making it difficult for individuals to relax and enjoy a sense of normalcy in their daily lives. Moreover, this fear can manifest in avoidance behaviors, as individuals may choose to isolate themselves or keep their distance from people of different races for fear of the unknown. These patterns of social avoidance can exacerbate feelings of loneliness, contributing to a downward spiral of negative mental health outcomes.

Additionally, White fear can damage White people's ability to form meaningful and fulfilling social relationships. Fear often leads to an "us versus them" mentality, pitting White individuals against people of color. This mindset, fueled by stereotypes and media narratives, can hinder genuine connections with individuals from diverse backgrounds. The fear of being perceived as racist can lead to excessive caution and self-censorship, making it difficult for White people to engage in open and honest conversations about race. As a result, they may miss out on valuable opportunities for growth, empathy, and personal development. Relationships founded on fear and mistrust are unlikely to foster the understanding and collaboration necessary for a harmonious and inclusive society.

White fear damages more than White people's mental health and social dynamics; White fear can impede the personal growth of White individuals. Fear often operates as a barrier to change and progress, promoting a conservative and defensive mindset. For White people, this may mean clinging to outdated beliefs and resisting efforts toward greater equality and social justice. The fear of losing power and privilege can hinder the ability to reflect on one's own biases critically and work toward dismantling systems of oppression. By succumbing to fear, White people are deprived of the opportunity to contribute to a more equitable society, instead perpetuating harmful notions of racial superiority and perpetuating existing inequities.

White Fatigue

White fatigue highlights the challenges associated with confronting and unlearning systemic racism. In recent years, there has been a growing awareness and discussion surrounding race, privilege, and social justice issues. As these conversations have gained traction, a phenomenon known as "White fatigue" has emerged. White fatigue refers to the exhaustion and resentment experienced by some White individuals when confronted with the realities of systemic racism, leading them to perceive themselves as victims.

White fatigue can be seen as a response to the profound changes taking place in societies where marginalized voices are increasingly being amplified. As topics of racial justice and equality are brought to the forefront, some White individuals may find their preconceived notions challenged and their privileges scrutinized. Consequently, they may experience discomfort, defensiveness, and fatigue as their status quo is questioned.

White fatigue may come from White people's concerns about losing their unearned White privileges. One of the fundamental causes of White fatigue is the recognition that some societal advantages or privileges they have enjoyed were unearned due to their racial background. This realization might lead to feelings of guilt, shame, and disillusionment. Another negative consequence of White fatigue can be related to the psychological concept of cognitive dissonance, wherein individuals experience discomfort when their behaviors or beliefs clash with new information. Recognizing the existence of systemic racism contradicts the idea of a meritocracy, leading to cognitive dissonance among some White people.

For White people, they may feel that they are born to be blamed because they are White. The fear of being blamed may interweave with White fatigue to further contribute to White people's anxiety about being blamed or held responsible for societal injustices. Some White individuals may fear that their collective identification with patterns of inequality could result in personal attacks or accusations of complicity.

White fatigue may cause emotional distress or discomfort for some individuals; it is crucial to understand that such psychological distress may become hurdles for White people to develop their own identity. Some White people may believe that White fatigue may lead to an erosion of cultural heritage and a diluted sense of identity. However, it is essential to differentiate between recognizing the need for equality and cultural preservation. Engaging in anti-racist discourse does not necessitate erasure but rather an opportunity to understand and celebrate diversity.

White fatigue may damage White people's self-confidence about their racial identity and make them feel silenced or neglected. White fatigue can emerge as a response to feeling silenced or dismissed in conversations surrounding race. While creating inclusive spaces for discussions is important, it is equally important to acknowledge that historically marginalized groups have needed to fight for their voices to be heard.

White Vulnerability

White vulnerability refers to the condition in which White individuals experience vulnerability, often due to issues of race that challenge their power and privilege. While the historical trajectory places White people at the top of social hierarchies, the emergence of multiculturalism and intersectionality has increasingly highlighted the vulnerabilities experienced by other racial, ethnic, and marginalized groups. Nevertheless, it is crucial to recognize that White vulnerability exists within a distinct context, influenced by intersectional factors and societal structures.

White vulnerability is rooted in the intersection of race, privilege, and power dynamics. Historically, it arises from the fear of losing societal dominance, discomfort with increasing diversity, and threats to institutional hegemony. White individuals may feel vulnerable due to the dismantling of unearned advantages and privileges associated with their racial identity. Encountering a challenge to their supremacy often elicits defensiveness and resistance, perpetuating damaging ideologies.

Thus, White vulnerability can have profound psychological, emotional, and social consequences for White individuals. The fear of losing racial privileges and the sense of being threatened can lead to a siege mentality and defensive behavior. This can manifest as resentment, anger, or scapegoating of other racial groups. Additionally, White vulnerability can hinder personal growth, preventing individuals from fully understanding and appreciating different cultures, perspectives, and lived experiences outside their own.

White vulnerability can extend beyond individual experiences and affect entire communities. When large segments of White society feel threatened, it can lead to the formation of closed communities and echo chambers, where misinformation and conspiracy theories thrive. This can have detrimental effects on social cohesion, foster division, and promote extremist ideologies. White vulnerability, if unchecked, can also undermine efforts toward inclusivity, perpetuating systemic racism and hindering societal progress.

Chapter 2

Historical Landmark

It is a long road to transfer from racial discrimination to racial inclusion. The transition might have already been started by those anti-racism pioneers and fighters hundreds of years ago, and fortunately or unfortunately, the transition journey is still ongoing. As Lao Tzu said in Dao De Jing, "A journey of a thousand miles begins with a single step." Even a long and daunting journey of transforming racial discrimination into racial inclusion, the critical point is about the starting point of transformation, such as the civil rights movement or something that begins with one first step.

The transition toward racial inclusion is a collective transformation shared by people across different racial groups rather than being the sole responsibility of a specific racial group. As racism and White supremacy damage people's mental health across different races, racial inclusion requires the efforts of people from various racial backgrounds. People from each racial background would experience the positive impacts of racial inclusion.

To discuss racial inclusion, it is essential to acknowledge the historical significance of civil rights, as well as the movements, events, and actions that have aimed to combat racism from people of different races (e.g., Black people and White people). The historical landmark goes beyond merely recording past events; it serves as a testament to the endeavors, sacrifices, failures, and triumphs of individuals who have relentlessly fought against racial discrimination, propelling the path toward progress. Importantly, historical landmarks demonstrate people's change from racial discrimination into racial inclusion and inspire people to redefine the meanings of racial discrimination and racial inclusion.

FROM JIM CROW LAWS IN 1896 TO THE CIVIL RIGHTS ACT OF 1964

It took 68 years to overturn the Jim Crow laws. The Jim Crow laws were a series of state and local laws enacted in the United States between 1876 and 1964. These laws were designed to enforce racial segregation and reinforce White supremacy in the South. The term "Jim Crow" derives from a character in minstrel shows prevalent in the late nineteenth century, in which White performers would portray Black people in exaggerated and demeaning ways. These laws profoundly impacted American society, affecting every aspect of life, including education. This chapter explores the history of the Jim Crow laws, their impact on graduate school education, and their lasting effects on the pursuit of educational equality.

The Jim Crow laws had a particularly detrimental impact on education for Black people, especially at the graduate school level. Under these laws, segregated schools became the norm, with separate facilities, resources, and curricula for Black and White students. While White schools received more funding and support, Black schools were neglected, vastly under-resourced, and often staffed by underqualified teachers. This stark educational inequality perpetuated a cycle of limited opportunities for Black students, limiting their prospects for graduate school education or higher education (Brown, 2006).

Graduate schools, including law schools and medical schools, were not exempt from segregation under the Jim Crow laws. Black students who aspired to pursue professional degrees faced significant obstacles. Most leading institutions refused to admit black students, and those that did often imposed higher admission standards or limited enrollment to token numbers. For example, medical schools like the University of Virginia and the University of Alabama enforced racially discriminatory practices, effectively barring black students from pursuing careers in medicine.

Worse, segregated graduate schools not only limited access but also offered fewer opportunities for black students to engage in higher-level studies. Those who managed to enroll often encountered limited course offerings in comparison to their White counterparts. Black students were often excluded from advanced courses, seminars, or research opportunities. Such limitations hindered their ability to gain the skills and knowledge required to compete at the highest level in their respective fields, perpetuating educational inequalities and limiting opportunities for career advancement.

The segregation in graduate school also impacts Black students' career prospects. Denied access to professional schools, they faced severe barriers to entry into prestigious careers such as medicine, law, academia, and other highly skilled professions. The lack of Black professionals in these fields, particularly in leadership and decision-making positions, further perpetuated systemic racial discrimination and limited upward mobility for African American communities.

Thus, the Jim Crow laws left an indelible mark on American society, including the educational system. The segregation and discrimination they enforced deprived Black people of equal access to graduate school education and consequently limited opportunities for professional advancement. While progress has been made through legislative changes and civil rights activism, the legacy of the Jim Crow laws continues to impact educational opportunities for marginalized communities, highlighting the ongoing need for equitable access to education at all levels for all individuals.

Despite the negative consequences and limitations of the Jim Crow laws, in the mid-twentieth century, the civil rights movement gained momentum, demanding an end to racial segregation and discrimination in all areas of society, including education. The landmark Supreme Court decision in *Brown v. Board of Education* in 1954 declared that segregated educational facilities were unconstitutional. However, it took years of legislative changes, legal challenges, and grassroots activism to fully dismantle the Jim Crow laws and their effects on education.

BROWN V. BOARD IN 1954

The landmark Supreme Court case *Brown v. Board of Education* in 1954 was a pivotal moment in American history in education and a significant turning point in the fight for civil rights. It is important to know the background of the case, the legal arguments presented, and the implications and impacts of the Court's decision on education in the United States.

Brown v. Board of Education emerged from lawsuits that challenged the constitutionality of racial segregation in public schools. The National Association for the Advancement of Colored People (NAACP) filed the initial case on behalf of Linda Brown, a young African American girl from Topeka, Kansas. The NAACP argued that segregation of public schools based on race, as practiced in Topeka and many other states, violated the Equal Protection Clause of the Fourteenth Amendment.

The legal arguments presented in *Brown v. Board of Education* centered around two main questions: whether "separate but equal" facilities for Black and White students were genuinely equal and whether segregation inherently damaged the self-esteem and psychological well-being of African American children. Psychologists Kenneth and Mamie Clark demonstrated that segregation harmed Black children's self-images (Clark & Clark, 1939). Their testimony before the Supreme Court contributed to the landmark Supreme Court case that desegregated American public schools: *Brown v. Board of*

Education of Topeka, Kansas. Moreover, the NAACP contended that segregation resulted in inherently unequal conditions, arguing that Black schools were consistently underfunded, lacked resources, and offered inferior education compared to their White counterparts. Expert witnesses were called in to testify about these disparities, providing empirical evidence to challenge the notion of equality under segregation.

The segregation also had a detrimental psychological impact on Black children. They presented evidence that racial segregation perpetuated feelings of inferiority and stigmatization among African American students, hampering their ability to learn and impeding their future success. The psychological research used during the trial helped shape the understanding of the long-term harms of racially segregated classrooms. In a unanimous decision, the Supreme Court ruled in favor of the plaintiffs in *Brown v. Board of Education*, declaring that state laws establishing separate public schools for Black and White students violated the Equal Protection Clause of the Fourteenth Amendment. On May 17, 1954, US Supreme Court chief justice Earl Warren delivered the unanimous ruling in the landmark civil rights case *Brown v. Board of Education of Topeka, Kansas*. He famously stated that "separate educational facilities are inherently unequal" (Clark, 1979, p. 477).

The decision in *Brown v. Board of Education* had far-reaching consequences for education and the broader civil rights movement in the United States. Desegregation efforts gained momentum, and subsequent court cases further challenged segregation in other aspects of public life. The ruling inspired activists and laid the foundation for the Civil Rights Act of 1964 and the Voting Rights Act of 1965.

One immediate effect was the dismantling of legal segregation in schools. While resistance to integration was prevalent in many Southern states, gradual progress culminated in significant changes in the 1970s and 1980s. The number of African American students attending predominantly White schools increased, and the overall quality of education for minority students improved.

The decision also had implications beyond education. It marked a turning point in the fight against racial discrimination and inspired other marginalized groups to take legal action against systemic injustice. The ruling brought the issue of civil rights to the forefront of American consciousness, sparking discussions about equality and justice that continue to this day. Thus, *Brown v. Board of Education* was a watershed moment in American history, effectively declaring racial segregation in public education unconstitutional. By rejecting the doctrine of "separate but equal," the Court recognized the inherent inequality and harm caused by segregation. Although challenges and resistance persisted, the ruling set a milestone example of equality and justice in education.

A TRAGIC BUT HISTORICAL LANDMARK: ASSASSINATION OF DR. MARTIN LUTHER KING JR.

At 6:05 p.m. on Thursday, April 4, 1968, a sorrowful moment occurred when Dr. Martin Luther King Jr. was shot dead while standing on a balcony outside his second-floor room at the Lorraine Motel in Memphis, Tennessee. News of Dr. King's assassination prompted significant impacts on this country. During Dr. King's funeral, a tape recording played in which he expressed how he wanted to be remembered after his death. He said, "I'd like somebody to mention that day that Martin Luther King Jr., tried to give his life serving others" (King, 1968).

After the assassination, it shows that although people tend to focus on the impact of his work during his life, they often neglect the effect of his death on racial discrimination and racial inclusion. Dr. King's death may impact people across different races in at least two ways. First, sadly, his death may shatter the dreams of Black people who pursue a life with equality and justice. The traumatic nightmare of broken dreams may further make Black people feel deeply disappointed while mourning the most significant loss in history. For Black people, Dr. King's assassination represents the punishment for being someone as peaceful and human as King could be. Second, not only for Black people but for White people, Dr. King's assassination was a life-awakening experience.

The Impact of the Assassination of Dr. Martin Luther King Jr.

The assassination of Dr. Martin Luther King had a profound impact on American society, particularly in the realms of civil rights, social justice, and race relations. Dr. King's assassination not only marked the tragic loss of one of the most influential figures in American history, but it also sparked a wave of change that reshaped the course of the nation.

The immediate impact of Dr. King's assassination was one of shock, grief, and anger. Riots broke out in more than 100 cities across America, leading to widespread destruction and violence. The assassination also temporarily halted progress on civil rights legislation, as many questioned the effectiveness of nonviolent protest in the face of such a tragic event. However, the leadership vacuum left by Dr. King's death ultimately led to a shift in the civil rights movement. With his voice silenced, other leaders emerged, such as Jesse Jackson and Andrew Young, who pursued more confrontational approaches to advocate for racial equality. This paved the way for the Black Power movement and the rise of more radical factions within the Black community.

Impact on the African American Community

Dr. King's assassination had a profound effect on the African American community. While it initially engendered anger and despair, it also created a greater sense of unity and resilience. The assassination served as a rallying point, reinforcing the importance of continued efforts to combat racism, discrimination, and inequality. Moreover, Dr. King's assassination highlighted the need for African Americans to engage in political activism and pursue leadership roles. This led to increased African American representation in politics, business, and academia as the community sought to create lasting change from within.

Impact on American Society

Dr. King's assassination had a far-reaching impact on American society. It served as a wake-up call, forcing the nation to confront its deep-seated racism and inequality. The following civil unrest highlighted the deep-rooted divisions within American society and underlined the need for genuine social change. The assassination also prompted a reevaluation of racial relations across the nation. It shattered the illusion of racial progress and led to a more critical examination of systemic racism and social injustice. This newfound awareness sparked discussions on racial inequality that continue to shape public discourse today.

The Civil Rights Division of the Department of Justice, established in 1957, is dedicated to safeguarding the civil and constitutional rights of all individuals in the United States. Congress established the Civil Rights Division in 1957 to protect the civil and constitutional rights of all Americans, especially those who are vulnerable. This Division is responsible for enforcing federal laws prohibiting discrimination based on race, color, sex, disability, religion, familial status, military status, and national origin.

CIVIL RIGHTS MOVEMENT WON'T DIE

Martin Luther King Jr.'s assassination marked a turning point in the Civil Rights Movement, challenging activists to continue the fight for justice and equality in new and creative ways. The movement forged ahead, fueled by the momentum generated during King's leadership, ultimately leading to significant legal, social, and cultural progress. However, the struggle for civil rights remains ongoing as the nation strives to address systemic racism, discrimination, and inequality. The legacy of Dr. King Jr. and the continued fight for justice serve as a reminder that the pursuit of equal rights is an ongoing journey that requires vigilance and unwavering commitment.

One influential movement that emerged in response to King's death was the Black Power movement. With its emphasis on racial pride, self-determination, and community empowerment, this movement sought to shift the narrative surrounding Blacks. It encouraged the exploration of African heritage and culture, promoting self-sufficiency and the establishment of black-controlled institutions. Although some criticized the Black Power movement for its confrontational tactics, it brought attention to the unique experiences and struggles faced by the black community. In addition to the Black Power movement, more and more activities and critical thinking joined together to reinforce the legacy of Dr. King Jr. and to further strengthen the impact of the civil rights movement.

In sum, history is replete with stories of resilience and resistance in the face of racial discrimination. African Americans, alongside White allies and civil rights organizations, fought ardently against Jim Crow laws. The landmark case, *Brown v. Board of Education*, led to the Supreme Court's ruling that segregated public schools were unconstitutional. This decision, coupled with the Civil Rights Movement spearheaded by leaders like Martin Luther King Jr., significantly challenged Jim Crow laws' legitimacy and eventually paved the way for their repeal. Thus, even after the tragic and violent assassination of Dr. King Jr., there were more milestone activities and movements to promote social justice.

From the Jim Crow laws to the Civil Rights Movement, there were many profound political impacts, paving the way for the passage of landmark legislation that promoted equality and civil rights. Arguably, the most notable achievement was the Civil Rights Act of 1964, which prohibited discrimination based on race, color, religion, sex, or national origin. This act eliminated legal segregation in public places, leading to more equitable employment practices. Additionally, there were other impacts related to the Civil Rights Movement:

Educational Impact. The Civil Rights Movement also made significant strides in challenging racial inequality within the education system. Prior to this movement, schools were segregated, with African American students confined to underfunded and inferior facilities. The landmark Supreme Court case, *Brown v. Board of Education* in 1954, led to the desegregation of public schools and dismantled the pernicious "separate but equal" doctrine in education.

Social Impact. One must recognize the social impact of the Civil Rights Movement. The movement created a powerful collective consciousness, sparking national civil rights and equality discourse. People of all races, ethnicities, and backgrounds were mobilized to support the cause, forming various civil rights organizations like the Southern Christian Leadership Conference (SCLC) and the Student Nonviolent Coordinating Committee

(SNCC). These organizations galvanized millions to protest peacefully, raising widespread awareness and challenging societal norms, ultimately dismantling the barriers of racial segregation and discrimination.

Economic Impact. The Civil Rights Movement also indelibly impacted the economic opportunities available to African Americans. By demanding equal rights and economic justice, the movement contributed to the increased representation of African Americans in the workforce, fairer wages, and improved labor conditions. Moreover, the movement prompted companies to adopt non-discrimination policies and diverse hiring practices, challenging the prevailing racist hiring practices of the time.

Legislative Impact. The Civil Rights Movement also spurred the rise of African American political representation. Activists like Martin Luther King Jr., Fannie Lou Hamer, and John Lewis were instrumental in pushing for legislative changes while inspiring a new generation of African American leaders. As a result, there was a significant increase in the number of African Americans elected to political offices, ensuring their voices were heard and their interests represented in government.

In addition to the impacts of the civil rights movements and Dr. King Jr.'s legacy, there were other critical changes that promoted the power of change in advancing anti-racism and social justice.

THE RISE OF ANTI-RACISM EXERCISE

Anti-racism exercises could be tools to transform racial discrimination into racial inclusion.

Blue Eyes/Brown Eyes Anti-racism Exercise

Many White Americans were shocked, sad, or angry at Dr. King's assassination. One of the responses was the "Blue Eyes/Brown Eyes Anti-Racism Exercise" (Elliott, 1968).

The Blue Eyes/Brown Eyes anti-racism exercise is a revolutionary teaching tool that aims to shed light on the impact of racial discrimination and promote inclusivity in educational institutions. Developed by Jane Elliott, a renowned American educator and diversity trainer, the exercise has been widely recognized for its transformative effects. The following paragraphs will critically examine the effectiveness of the Blue Eyes/Brown Eyes exercise in addressing racism and fostering social change.

The Blue Eyes/Brown Eyes exercise was initially conducted in a third-grade classroom in 1968. Following the assassination of Dr. Martin Luther King Jr., Elliott developed the exercise to help young children understand the harmful consequences of racial discrimination through direct experience. Gradually, the exercise attracted attention beyond its initial classroom setting due to its profound impact on children and adults. This exercise raises the following five points.

First, the Blue Eyes/Brown Eyes exercise promoted the development of critical consciousness. One of the primary outcomes of the Blue Eyes/Brown Eyes exercise is the development of critical consciousness regarding racism. By dividing participants into two groups based on eye color and attributing superiority to one group, the exercise provides a platform for experiencing discrimination firsthand. This immersion enables participants to empathize with marginalized individuals and reflect on the inherent injustices that permeate society. In a graduate education context, this exercise can provoke deep introspection among students, challenging their preconceived notions and biases and fostering a more comprehensive understanding of racial injustices.

Second, the Blue Eyes/Brown Eyes exercise enhances empathy and understanding between people from different races/ethnicities. The Blue Eyes/Brown Eyes exercise facilitates empathy and understanding. Regardless of their eye color, participants are exposed to the oppressive dynamics created by the exercise. By experiencing these dynamics, individuals can better comprehend the systemic nature of racism and its repercussions. This heightened understanding can cultivate empathy among graduate students, leading to a more inclusive educational environment that values diversity, encourages dialogue, and promotes understanding.

Third, the Blue Eyes/Brown Eyes exercise challenges people's implicit biases. Implicit bias, or unconscious stereotypes toward specific groups, is pervasive and often influences decision-making processes. Implicit bias has been prevalent among White people's colorblind racial attitudes toward BIPOC. The Blue Eyes/Brown Eyes exercise helps challenge these implicit biases by making them overt and visible. When participants engage in discriminatory behaviors and attitudes based on assigned eye color, it becomes apparent how subtle biases can be internalized and perpetuated. This exercise prompts students to reflect on their own biases in a graduate education setting. It compels them to confront and challenge these biases for personal growth and to become agents of change.

Fourth, the Blue Eyes/Brown Eyes exercise highlights cognitive dissonance and transformative learning. The Blue Eyes/Brown Eyes exercise invokes cognitive dissonance, a psychological state where inconsistencies between beliefs and experiences create tension. This tension often leads to transformative learning, as individuals are compelled to reconcile their preexisting understanding of racial inequality with the vivid, firsthand experience of discrimination. Graduate students experience transformative learning through active engagement in the exercise, causing them to reevaluate their beliefs, behaviors, and perceptions of race.

Fifth, the Blue Eyes/Brown Eyes exercise promotes allies and advocacy. Even though this exercise was developed more than half a century ago, the Blue Eyes/Brown Eyes exercise still offers a stepping stone toward becoming allies in the fight against racial discrimination. By experiencing discrimination and acknowledging its impact, educators and practitioners can develop the motivation and skills necessary to advocate for change within their professional spheres. This exercise serves as a catalyst for graduate students to actively promote anti-racist initiatives, challenge institutional practices, and contribute to the creation of an equitable society.

A CRITICAL STEP OF RACIAL INCLUSION: WHITE PEOPLE JOIN ANTI-RACISM

White people joining the anti-racism movement represents a significant shift in the dynamics of fighting against racism. Their participation is pivotal in creating a society that fosters equality, justice, and inclusivity. They bring unique perspectives, resources, and networks that can effectively challenge racist ideologies and dismantle systemic oppression. By educating themselves, confronting their biases, and actively advocating for racial justice, White individuals stand as catalysts for positive change. Together, united against racism, they contribute to a more equitable and harmonious society (Brown, 2002).

White Pioneers on Racial Inclusion

A history is made with countless people's stories. Some stories are well-known, and others are unknown or even forgotten by this world. Whether known or not, this section explores pioneers who left a legacy and impact on the journey of racial inclusion.

Virginia Foster Durr (1903–1999)

Virginia Foster Durr was a remarkable American civil rights activist, women's rights advocate, and writer who played a crucial role in advancing social justice in the United States. Her tireless efforts to combat racism, sexism, and poverty have left a lasting impact on American society and continue to inspire activists today. Below are brief highlights about Durr's life and work, underscoring her contributions to education and understanding at the research in education level.

Born in Birmingham, Alabama, in 1903, Virginia Foster Durr grew up in a society deeply entrenched in racial segregation and gender inequality.

However, she was raised in a progressive, open-minded family that influenced her worldview and ignited her commitment to social justice. Durr's father, Dr. Clifford Foster, was a physician who provided medical care to African Americans and actively supported civil rights causes. Her mother, Lucy Foster, was a suffragist who fought for women's right to vote.

Durr's early experiences witnessing the mistreatment of African Americans and the subjugation of women deeply impacted her and set the stage for her lifelong activism. She attended Wellesley College, a prestigious women's college in Massachusetts, where she studied sociology and was exposed to progressive ideas. This educational experience further solidified her belief in equality and justice for all.

Throughout her life, Durr was driven by a commitment to understanding and empathy. Her encounters and friendships with individuals from different races and backgrounds shaped her understanding of the injustices in American society. Durr recognized the importance of education in fostering understanding and breaking down barriers, and she made it her mission to promote education as a means of social and racial progress.

With her husband, Clifford Durr, a prominent lawyer and civil rights activist, Durr fought against racial segregation and discrimination in the South. They both played significant roles in supporting the Montgomery Bus Boycott led by Dr. Martin Luther King Jr. in 1955, providing financial and legal assistance to activists.

Durr's passion for education extended beyond her personal experiences and activism. In the 1960s, she began working with the Center for the Study of Democratic Institutions, which promotes civil rights, social justice, and human rights. Through this platform, Durr conducted extensive research on race relations in the United States and wrote several influential articles and papers that shed light on the deep-rooted causes of racism.

One of Durr's most significant contributions to education at the research thesis level was her collaboration with historian Howard Zinn. Together, they developed a groundbreaking research project to uncover the untold stories of ordinary people who had participated in the civil rights movement. Durr interviewed numerous activists and compiled their stories, providing an invaluable resource for future scholars and researchers.

Furthermore, Durr's memoir, *Outside the Magic Circle: The Autobiography of Virginia Foster Durr*, published in 1985, was a powerful educational tool. In her book, Durr candidly shared her experiences growing up amid segregation and her journey to becoming an advocate for racial and gender equality. This memoir provided valuable insights into the struggles and triumphs of the civil rights movement and inspired future activists to speak out against injustice.

In sum, Virginia Foster Durr was an exceptional individual who dedicated her life to advancing social justice and education. Her unwavering commitment to equality and her efforts to promote understanding continue to shape the field of research in education. By highlighting the importance of education in fostering empathy and breaking down barriers, Durr has left an indelible mark on American society, inspiring future generations to strive for a more just and inclusive world.

J. Waties Waring (1880–1968)

J. Waties Waring was a courageous and groundbreaking judge who played a significant role in advancing civil rights in the United States. Examining his life and contributions provides valuable insights into the struggles and triumphs of the civil rights movement and the impact of individual actors within the judicial system.

Waring was born on August 6, 1880, in Charleston, South Carolina, and belonged to a privileged White family. He received his education at prestigious institutions such as St. Paul's School in Concord, New Hampshire, and Harvard University. After completing his education, Waring returned to South Carolina to practice law. Initially, his legal career was unremarkable, primarily serving wealthy clients in his home state. However, this would change dramatically in the 1940s.

During this time, Waring began his transformation toward becoming an advocate for civil rights. He became disillusioned with the systemic racism that permeated the Southern legal system. Witnessing the pervasive discrimination and injustice experienced by African Americans in his community, Waring realized that change was desperately needed.

In 1942, President Franklin D. Roosevelt appointed Waring as a federal district judge for the District of South Carolina. In this position, Waring started challenging the status quo and using his power to fight against racial segregation. His most notable contribution came in 1951 when he presided over the case *Briggs v. Elliott*, a landmark school desegregation lawsuit.

At the time, racial segregation in South Carolina's public schools was enforced by law through the "separate but equal" doctrine established by *Plessy v. Ferguson*. However, Waring recognized the inherent inequality in segregated educational facilities and ruled that segregation itself was inherently unequal. His decision was considered groundbreaking, laying the foundation for future legal battles against segregation.

Despite being a southern White judge surrounded by racial hostility, Waring was unafraid to speak out against segregation. He faced severe backlash from his community, public officials, and even his family. He was ostracized and threatened, and ultimately, his wife divorced him due to his stance on civil rights. Nevertheless, Waring persevered, driven by his commitment to equality and justice.

Waring's dissenting opinions in several other cases further cemented his reputation as a champion of civil rights. He criticized the racial bias in the criminal justice system, the discriminatory practices of juries, and even the apathy of his colleagues in the judiciary. Waring's boldness and principled stands made him a beacon of hope for African Americans and progressive allies in the fight against Jim Crow laws.

While his rulings and opinions did not immediately overturn segregation, Waring's impact was significant and far-reaching. His fierce criticism of segregated education laid the groundwork for the Supreme Court's landmark decision in *Brown v. Board of Education* in 1954. The Court cited Waring's dissent as a major influence in rejecting the "separate but equal" doctrine and declaring racial segregation in schools unconstitutional.

Waring's legacy goes beyond the decisions he made on the bench. His courage and unwavering dedication to justice leave an indelible mark on the civil rights movement. By openly challenging long-held beliefs and advocating for equal rights for all, regardless of race, Waring inspired others to join the fight against segregation and discrimination.

Moreover, Waring's personal transformation from a privileged White man to a fervent advocate for civil rights demonstrates the power of individual growth in fostering societal change. His journey serves as a valuable reminder that even those who benefit from systemic injustices can become allies and agents of change.

Taken together, J. Waties Waring's contributions to civil rights in the United States were invaluable. Through his groundbreaking rulings and vocal dissents, he helped pave the way for desegregation and the dismantling of Jim Crow laws. Waring's personal journey from a privileged background to a champion for racial equality stands as an example of how individuals can challenge and change their own perspectives and society at large. His unwavering commitment to justice and fearless pursuit of equality makes him a significant figure in the history of civil rights in America.

Anne McCarty Braden (1924–2006)

Anne McCarty Braden, born in 1924, was an American civil rights activist and journalist who dedicated her life to fighting against racial inequality and promoting social justice. Recognized for her fearless commitment to racial equality, Braden played a significant role in challenging institutionalized racism and advocating for the rights of African Americans. It is crucial to highlight her contributions to the Civil Rights Movement, her journalistic efforts, and her enduring legacy in the pursuit of social equality. Anne McCarty Braden was born on July 28, 1924, in Louisville, Kentucky, a state notorious for its deep-seated racism and segregation. Growing up in a racially divided society, Braden witnessed firsthand the injustices endured by Black

Americans, which profoundly impacted her worldview. Her awareness and empathy for the struggles faced by African Americans became the foundation for her future transformative activism.

Obtaining her bachelor's degree in journalism from the University of Louisville, Braden began her career as a journalist. While working as a reporter for the Louisville Times, she became active in the Civil Rights Movement in the 1950s. Often collaborating with her husband, Carl Braden, she sought to challenge segregationist policies and promote racial integration in the South.

Anne Braden rose to prominence due to her involvement in the Southern Conference Educational Fund (SCEF), an organization established to combat racism in the southern United States. Serving as SCEF's publicity director, Braden brought attention to the racial inequality and oppression faced by African Americans. She garnered support for the organization, both nationally and internationally, ensuring it was at the forefront of the fight for civil rights.

One defining moment in Braden's life was her arrest and trial following the purchase of a house for an African American couple, Andrew and Charlotte Wade, in an all-White neighborhood in 1954. Braden and her husband were charged with sedition, a charge historically reserved for individuals promoting treason. The trial garnered significant media attention, helping expose the divisive patterns of segregation and racism that persisted in America. Although Braden was acquitted, the trial served as a catalyst, further invigorating her commitment to the civil rights cause.

As a journalist, Braden utilized her writing skills to expose systemic racism and promote dialogue on racial inequality. She coauthored the book *The Wall Between* with her husband, which reflected on their journey and the harsh reality of segregation. Her commitment to journalism became an integral part of her activism and allowed her to reach a wider audience, spreading the ideals of equality, justice, and anti-racism principles.

Following the turbulent years of the Civil Rights Movement, Braden remained active in addressing the lingering racial disparities and advocating for social justice. She co-founded the National Anti-Klan Network, an organization dedicated to combating White supremacy and Klan violence. Braden's legacy serves as a constant reminder of the need for continued efforts toward social justice.

In conclusion, Anne McCarty Braden's life was characterized by an unwavering commitment to racial equality and social justice. Her role as a civil rights activist and journalist not only challenged oppressive systems but also exposed racial injustices to a wider audience. Through her steadfast advocacy, Braden inspired countless individuals to question the status quo and strive for a more inclusive society. Her legacy serves as a guiding light for future generations in the pursuit of equality, justice, and social change.

Herbert R. Kohl (born 1937)

Herbert R. Kohl is a writer and educator from New York City who authored *36 Children* and 25 other books about education and civil rights. Herbert R. Kohl is a renowned educator, author, and advocate for progressive education. Throughout his career, he has made significant contributions to the field of education, particularly in the areas of critical pedagogy, multicultural education, and alternative teaching methods. His work has had a profound impact on educational theory and practice, promoting student-centered learning and fostering a love for learning in students. Here are highlights about the life and work of Herbert R. Kohl, exploring his ideas, writings, and accomplishments.

Herbert R. Kohl was born on August 22, 1937, in Newark, New Jersey. Raised in a Jewish family, he experienced firsthand the impacts of anti-Semitism and discrimination. These early experiences shaped his understanding of education as a means to empower individuals and challenge social inequalities. Kohl's educational journey started when he pursued a Bachelor of Arts degree in English at Harvard University. While at Harvard, he became interested in education and took on various teaching roles in schools and community centers, working with low-income and minority students.

Kohl's experiences in these settings exposed him to the challenges faced by marginalized students who often did not have access to quality education. This led him to question traditional educational approaches and seek alternative methods to engage students and foster their love for learning. His early observations and experiences served as the foundation for his educational philosophy, which centers around empowering students and valuing their voices and experiences.

One of Kohl's most significant contributions to education is his advocacy for critical pedagogy. He believes that education should not be limited to the transmission of facts and skills but should instead encourage critical thinking, creativity, and social activism. Critical pedagogy challenges the existing power structures in the classroom and supports students in developing their own voices and perspectives. By encouraging students to question and analyze the world around them, Kohl believes that education can become a tool for social change.

In addition to critical pedagogy, Kohl is also known for his work in multicultural education. He argues that education should acknowledge and celebrate the diverse backgrounds and experiences of students. By integrating multicultural perspectives into the curriculum, teachers can create an inclusive and supportive learning environment that promotes mutual respect and understanding. Kohl's writings on multicultural education, including his book *Should We Burn Babar? Essays on Children's Literature and the Power of Stories*, have been influential in promoting a more inclusive and diverse approach to teaching (Kohl, 1996).

Kohl has also been a strong advocate for alternative teaching methods. He promotes experiential and hands-on learning, where students are actively engaged in their education. Kohl believes that traditional educational approaches, which often prioritize rote memorization and passive learning, do not take into account the unique needs and interests of individual students. In his book *The Open Classroom: A Practical Guide for Teachers*, Kohl (1969) provides practical ideas and strategies for creating an open and interactive learning environment where students are encouraged to explore their interests and learn at their own pace.

Throughout his career, Kohl has received numerous awards and honors for his contributions to education. He has written several books, including *36 Children* (Kohl, 1967) and *I Won't Learn from You: And Other Thoughts on Creative Maladjustment* (Kohl, 1991), in which he shares his experiences as a teacher and advocate for progressive education. Kohl has also worked closely with various educational organizations, including the National Association for Multicultural Education and Teachers College at Columbia University.

Finally, Herbert R. Kohl has been a transformative figure in the field of education, advocating for student-centered learning, multicultural education, and alternative teaching methods. His ideas have challenged traditional educational approaches and have had a profound impact on educational theory and practice. By championing critical pedagogy and valuing the voices and experiences of students, Kohl has sought to make education a tool for social change and empowerment. As educators continue to grapple with issues of equality and inclusivity, Kohl's work remains highly relevant and offers valuable insights into creating more effective and meaningful educational experiences for all students.

Legacy of White Anti-racism Pioneers

The above White pioneers on anti-racism are a few models showing us how to promote racial inclusion across races/ethnicities. The fight against racism has gained significant momentum in recent years, calling for an end to systemic discrimination and social injustice across various societies. While racial minorities such as Black people have been at the forefront of this movement, an increasing number of White individuals have also started joining forces to collectively combat racism. From these pioneers, we learn several key issues to make the historical landmark of racial inclusion more powerful.

Awareness and Empathy. A significant catalyst driving White people to join the anti-racism movement is the growing awareness and empathy toward the lived experiences of racial minorities. Through exposure to diverse perspectives, personal experiences, and education, White individuals often gain insight into the systemic inequalities faced by marginalized communities. This increased awareness fosters empathy, leading them to acknowledge their privilege and recognize the need for collective action against racism.

Moral Imperative and Social Justice. Embracing anti-racism goes beyond empathizing with marginalized communities. It stems from a moral imperative to reject racist ideologies and work toward a fair, just, and inclusive society. White individuals who join the anti-racism movement view racial equality as a fundamental human right and believe in actively dismantling oppressive systems. They recognize that by remaining silent or complicit, they perpetuate racial inequality and hinder progress toward a more egalitarian society.

Personal Growth and Healing. Taking part in the anti-racism movement allows White individuals the opportunity for personal growth and healing. It provides a space to confront their own biases, unlearn racist behaviors, and challenge deep-seated prejudices. Engaging in anti-racist education, workshops, and dialogues enables them to dismantle internalized racism and contribute to personal healing. By denouncing racism, White individuals take a crucial step toward creating healthier relationships and contributing to positive social change.

Allyship and Solidarity. White allies play a vital role in fostering racial justice movements. By joining anti-racism initiatives, they offer vital support to communities affected by racism. White individuals have a responsibility to use their privilege to amplify the voices of marginalized individuals, becoming influential allies in the struggle for equity. Leveraging their social capital, financial resources, and networks, White allies can help challenge discriminatory policies, advocate for equal representation, and promote inclusive narratives.

Improving the Efficacy of the Movement. A diverse and inclusive movement is more likely to dismantle the entrenched systemic racism that pervades society. The involvement of White individuals in the anti-racism movement adds weight, legitimacy, and credibility to the cause. By amplifying their voices, White allies can influence their peers, family members, and communities—an essential aspect given that dismantling racism requires collective action. White activists can utilize their platforms to influence policy changes, impact legislation, and create systemic reforms to achieve racial justice.

Chapter 3

Transformation

From Racial Discrimination to Racial Inclusion

Unlike Malcolm X, who initially viewed Whites as having no moral conscience and America as a nightmare that was doomed for its crimes of slavery and segregation, King possessed a redemptive faith in the goodness of White people. He insisted on loving White people despite their treatment of Black people, and he spoke of having a dream that Americans of all racial backgrounds could live in peace and goodwill.

However, Malcolm X's perspectives on White people were complex and evolved greatly throughout his life. During his early years within the Nation of Islam (NOI), Malcolm X harbored a deep-seated resentment toward White people. This perspective aligned with the NOI's teachings, which portrayed White people as inherently evil and the source of all problems faced by African Americans. Malcolm X's public speeches during this stage often contained confrontational rhetoric, advocating for the separation of races and espousing a strong anti-White sentiment. This radical phase reflected his personal experiences growing up in a racially segregated society and experiencing firsthand the brutality of racial discrimination.

In 1964, Malcolm X's perspective took a significant shift following his pilgrimage to Mecca, a transformative experience that exposed him to global perspectives on race and religion. During his journey, Malcolm X met Muslims of various races, including White Muslims, who displayed kindness, acceptance, and genuine brotherhood. This encounter shattered his previous black-and-white view of the world, prompting him to reevaluate his stance on White people.

After disassociating himself from the NOI, Malcolm X embarked on a journey of intellectual growth and self-discovery. He started to embrace the possibility of collaboration and allyship with White activists who shared the same values of racial equality and social justice. His evolving perspective recognized that the battle against racism required a unified effort, transcending racial divides. This shift is particularly evident in his discussions with civil rights leaders such as Martin Luther King Jr., with whom he explored avenues for cooperation.

Malcolm X's evolving perspective on White people remains a cornerstone of his legacy. By acknowledging the complexity and shades of gray in human interactions, he broke away from the rigid binary thinking prevalent in both Black nationalist and White supremacist ideologies. His later views emphasized the importance of building bridges between different races and fostering solidarity in the pursuit of social justice. Malcolm X's ability to evolve and question his own beliefs serves as a powerful example of the capacity for growth and understanding inherent in the human experience.

In sum, Malcolm X's perspectives on White people experienced a profound transformation throughout his life. From his early radicalism rooted in the NOI's teachings to his realization of the potential for interracial collaboration and allyship, his journey highlights the complexity and evolution of his thinking. By questioning his own beliefs and embracing the possibility of unity, Malcolm X positioned himself as a catalyst for change and understanding.

This book applies his journey of change as the foundation to explore the transformation from racial discrimination to racial inclusion. However, because racism-related stress and racial trauma significantly damage BIPOC well-being and cause them to struggle with PTSD and other psychological distress, it is critical that the transformation starts with racial healing for BIPOC individuals and communities.

Racism also damages the physical and mental health of White people by causing them to be defensive, anxious, avoidant, self-doubt, guilty, fearful, fatigued, and vulnerable when discussing race-related topics (Spanierman & Heppner, 2004). Thus, it is critical for White people that the transformation from racial discrimination to racial inclusion also begins with healing.

HEALING IN TRANSFORMATION

Although BIPOC and White people suffer the negative consequences of racism, they experience different symptoms. Thus, racial healing needs to be tailored to their experiences, symptoms, and cultural backgrounds. It is critical to define the healing process aligned with the contexts of the victims of racism. Thus, the healing should not be limited to individual healing and needs to include restructuring the policies and systems to reduce the disparities between BIPOC and White people. Below are detailed descriptions of healing in response to racism, which causes people physical, psychological, and emotional distress.

Recognizing Racial Trauma

Recognizing racial trauma is the first step to help victims of racism get healed. Recognizing racial trauma is crucial to promote healing, justice, and equality. A clear understanding and awareness of racial trauma involve acknowledging the historical context of racism, understanding its collective impact, and validating the experiences of BIPOC individuals. Racial healing acknowledges the historical and ongoing trauma experienced by marginalized communities as a result of racial injustices, discrimination, and the lingering effects of colonialism. It seeks to address these injustices through reconciliation, sociocultural understanding, and dialogue within communities and institutions. Racial healing acknowledges the power dynamics at play, works to challenge systemic oppression, and fosters opportunities for healing and empowerment.

Racial trauma refers to the psychological and emotional stress experienced by individuals as a result of exposure to racial discrimination, violence, and systemic racism. This phenomenon, which has historically targeted marginalized racial and ethnic groups, can leave long-lasting effects on physical, mental, and emotional well-being. Recognizing racial trauma is essential for addressing its impact and promoting a more inclusive and equitable society. While chapter 1 of this book describes the negative consequences of racism with four theories: the Generic Stress Model, the Biopsychosocial Model, the Race-based Traumatic Stress, and a Model of Integration of Racial Trauma and BIPOC's Strength, and how racism harms White people, this section focuses on strategies for recognizing racial trauma.

Identify the Source of Racial Discrimination

Identifying the source of racial discrimination is the first step to achieving racial trauma healing. As part of our collective responsibility to help victims get healed and to foster a more inclusive and equitable society, it is imperative to identify the sources of racial discrimination. It is critical to provide a comprehensive guide on identifying these sources to empower individuals and institutions to combat racial discrimination effectively. Racial trauma can come directly from other people or can be experienced within a wider system, such as institutional racism and cultural racism. It can result of a direct racism-related experience, or it can be experienced indirectly or vicariously. For example, one might watch TV shows, movies, or events in which other people encounter racism.

Source One: *Individual Racism.* Recognizing individual racism requires one to be aware of how race and ethnicity can influence interactions and shape perceptions. Some cues to identify individual racism include derogatory comments, stereotypes, microaggressions, or discriminatory behavior toward individuals from specific racial or ethnic backgrounds.

Understanding that racism is not solely reliant on overt manifestations but can also be subtle and unconscious is crucial. Additionally, racial trauma can be transmitted generationally, perpetuating the impact on individuals and communities.

Source Two: *Institutional Racism*. Institutional racism encompasses discriminatory practices within established institutions, whether public or private, that perpetuate racial disparities. Identifying institutional racism involves scrutinizing policies, rules, regulations, and procedures that may unintentionally create barriers or disadvantages for specific racial or ethnic groups. An investigation of representation among staff, leadership positions, or decision-making bodies, as well as the allocation of resources, can offer valuable insights into the presence of institutional racism.

Source Three: *Structural Racism*. Structural racism refers to the systems, policies, and practices embedded within society that perpetuate racial inequalities and prevent marginalized groups from accessing equal opportunities. Spotting structural racism necessitates analyzing existing power dynamics and social, economic, or political inequalities and identifying any patterns of discrimination that disproportionately affect certain racial or ethnic groups. Disparities in employment, education, healthcare, housing, or incarceration rates are often indicators of deeply ingrained structural racism that need addressing.

Source Four: *Systemic Racism*. Systemic racism refers to the collective interplay of individual, structural, and institutional racism resulting in sustained racial inequities. Spotting systemic racism requires understanding historical contexts, analyzing long-standing patterns of discrimination, and assessing the impact of policies and practices over time. Examining educational achievement gaps, wealth disparities, or criminal justice system biases can help identify systemic racism deeply entrenched within society.

Source Five: *Racism in Legal Context*. Racial discrimination is also influenced by legal frameworks and institutional practices. Analyzing legislation, court cases, and policies pertaining to racial discrimination allows for the identification of systemic sources of discrimination. A legal context analysis can reveal gaps or inconsistencies in addressing racial discrimination, leading to opportunities for reform and change.

Source Six: *Racism in Community Voice and Lived Experiences*. Acknowledging and centering the narratives of affected communities is crucial in identifying the sources of racial discrimination. Researchers at the educational level should engage directly with community members and individuals who have experienced racial discrimination to gain firsthand insight into their lived experiences. In-depth interviews, focus groups, and ethnographic studies can serve as appropriate methods to gather such data, ensuring that marginalized voices are heard and respected.

Source Seven: *Racism across Generations.* The source of racial trauma can be transmitted intergenerationally, such as racial trauma going across several generations of BIPOC. Thus, racism could be rooted in centuries of systemic oppression, racial violence, and discrimination. Historical events such as slavery, colonization, segregation, and forced displacement have paved the way for intergenerational trauma. Moreover, ongoing systemic racism, racial profiling, and police brutality continue to contribute to the perpetuation of racial trauma in contemporary society. Recognizing these structural factors is crucial for addressing racial trauma effectively.

Thus, in addition to individual racism and intergenerational racism, another primary source of racial discrimination is structural racism. This form of discrimination operates within the frameworks of institutions and systems, perpetuating unequal treatment and outcomes for different racial groups. Institutions such as education, criminal justice, healthcare, and employment can exhibit structural racism through biased policies, practices, and decision-making. It is important and necessary to identify this source through comprehensive analyses of historical and current data, examining the ways in which institutions influence disparities among racial groups.

Source Eight: *Racism in Media Influence and Representation.* Media plays a crucial role in shaping public perception. Hence, the media's influence and the portrayal of racial groups can contribute significantly to racial discrimination. Researchers at the education level can analyze media content to identify the sources of racial bias, such as biased reporting, lack of representation, or perpetuating stereotypes. Furthermore, examining media platforms and ownership structures can shed light on the underlying mechanisms that contribute to racial discrimination.

Source Nine: *Racism in Historical Narratives and Colonial Legacy.* Examining historical narratives and the legacy of colonialism is crucial in understanding present-day racial discrimination. People across different races/ethnicities need to explore and understand the impact of historical events, such as slavery, colonization, and other forms of racial oppression, on contemporary racial disparities. Analysis can include examining colonial laws, policies, and social structures that perpetuated racial discrimination and continue to influence societies today.

Importantly, in the United States, BIPOC individuals are most vulnerable due to living under a system of White supremacy. Racism exists in Whiteness, including White supremacy, White privilege, colorblind racial attitudes, and White fragility.

Source Ten: *Racism in Intersectionality and Multiple Discrimination.* Intersectionality is a valuable framework when identifying the sources of racial discrimination. Individuals are not solely defined by their racial identity but also by other social categories such as gender, sexuality, disability, or socioeconomic status. The overlap of these identities magnifies the discrimination individuals may face. Researchers can employ intersectional analysis to understand how multiple forms of discrimination intersect and potentially exacerbate racial discrimination. That is, the sources of racial discrimination could be multiple sources, chronic (across years or generations), direct or vicarious, real happenings or in movies or fictional formats, and various levels of severity ranging from implicit biases to violent, life-threatening, traumatic experiences.

Taken together, because racism damages and harms BIPOC and White people's well-being, it is everyone's responsibility to identify the sources of racism. With a clear recognition of the sources of racism, we are ready to move on to heal racial trauma. By acknowledging the existence and sources of racism at various levels and in various formats, individuals can unmask its veiled forces and contribute to the creation of inclusive spaces where equality and justice thrive. The fight against racism requires collective efforts, continuous education, and a commitment to dismantling discriminatory practices and fostering societal transformation from racial discrimination to racial inclusion.

RACIAL TRAUMA HEALING

To move forward from racial discrimination to racial inclusion, after identifying the sources of racism, the next step is to heal racial trauma or racism-related stress. Addressing racial trauma requires a collective approach to facilitate healing and empowerment. Communities, organizations, and policymakers must work to dismantle systemic racism, create opportunities for restorative justice, and provide equitable resources. Creating spaces for dialogue, advocacy, and activism can empower individuals affected by racial trauma to reclaim their identities and promote social change.

Trauma-informed Care for Racism

In recent years, discussions surrounding racial healing and trauma-informed care have gained significant attention in the field of education. Recognizing the historical legacy of systemic racism and its impact on marginalized communities, the concept of racial healing encompasses efforts to address these injustices and promote unity, equity, and social justice. Similarly, trauma-informed care emphasizes the importance of understanding and responding to the effects of trauma on individuals, particularly within vulnerable populations. This section aims to explore the intersection of racial healing and trauma-informed care, with a specific focus on their significance and potential in transforming education systems to be more equitable and inclusive.

Trauma-informed care recognizes the profound impact of trauma on BIPOC overall well-being, including their physical, emotional, and psychological health. Trauma disproportionately affects marginalized communities, who often face systemic discrimination and violence. Trauma-informed care approaches aim to create safe, supportive, and empowering environments, enabling individuals to heal and thrive. It emphasizes an understanding of trauma's physiological and psychological effects, trauma-sensitive practices, and the fostering of resilience and healing.

Racial healing and trauma-informed care are interlinked as communities and individuals within marginalized populations often face both historical and ongoing racial trauma. Acknowledging this connection is crucial for implementing effective initiatives and practices within education systems. Combining racial healing and trauma-informed care in education provides a comprehensive framework that addresses the specific needs of marginalized people, fostering an inclusive environment where healing and growth can occur.

Implementing trauma-informed care and practices involves recognizing the signs and consequences of trauma, creating safe spaces for affected individuals, and promoting healing. This can include training educators and practitioners in trauma-informed practices, developing trauma-sensitive curricula, and incorporating restorative justice practices that address trauma and promote social-emotional well-being. By employing these strategies, schools can create environments that support academic success, authentic engagement, and positive societal change.

Making racial healing practices more powerful requires everyone from different races to address historical injustices and actively dismantle systemic racism. This involves the willingness to recognize the damages that racism, Whiteness, White privileges, and other race-related stressors have caused to people's well-being. Such awareness promotes diversity in institutions and systems and facilitates honest and open dialogues about race and racism. Racial healing initiatives foster healing and understanding, allowing individuals to challenge the perpetuation of racial trauma and establish compassionate and equitable learning environments.

White people's physical, psychological, and emotional health get damaged by racism, which causes their shame, fear, guilt, anxiety, confusion, vulnerability, and self-doubt. For example, White fragility may make White people uncomfortable or avoid talking about race-related issues. Some White people feel blamed and are afraid of making mistakes in their language and behaviors. Other White people may escape the conversations regarding race, or they may be defensive or silent.

To heal the negative consequences of racism on White people through trauma-informed care, it is important to change the question from "What's racism wrong with you?" to "What racism happened to you?" A trauma-informed care approach focuses on acknowledging the negative experiences caused by racism. It is also important to address the psychological distress in their situation in order to provide effective care with a healing orientation. Adopting trauma-informed practices to help White people deal with the hurts related to racism can potentially improve their engagement and reduce their denial or defensiveness. Trauma-informed care would be more effective in building a positive relationship with White people in the process of addressing the impacts of racism.

Healing Racial Discrimination with Mindfulness

Mindfulness is a powerful tool to enhance well-being and promote holistic positive feelings. Mindfulness, rooted in ancient Eastern philosophical traditions, has been adapted and incorporated into various secular settings, including educational institutions. Thus, the principles of mindfulness also promote people's sensitivity to identifying racial discrimination. Mindfulness can be described as the state of paying deliberate attention to the present moment without judgment. It involves grounding oneself in the here and now and cultivating an awareness of one's thoughts, emotions, and bodily sensations.

Internally, it is important to be mindful of the internal responses to racism and symptoms related to racial trauma with mindfulness. Being mindful helps achieve a deep understanding of its signs and symptoms. These may manifest differently among individuals but commonly include feelings of anxiety, depression, hypervigilance, low self-esteem, and a sense of constant threat. Physical symptoms may also emerge, such as headaches, sleep disturbances, and cardiovascular issues. Understanding these indicators is crucial for identifying and validating the experiences of those affected by racial trauma, as well as for developing appropriate interventions.

Research and clinical practice suggest that regular mindfulness practice positively impacts mental health by reducing stress, anxiety, and depressive symptoms. It fosters emotional resilience by enabling individuals to observe and acknowledge their emotions without being overwhelmed by them. By promoting a sense of internal calm and stability, mindfulness allows individuals to counteract the detrimental effects of stress and enhance their overall emotional well-being.

Mindfulness practice has been shown to enhance cognitive abilities, including attention, memory, and executive functioning. By training individuals to be fully present in the moment, mindfulness decreases mind-wandering and improves focus and concentration. It also encourages open-mindedness and flexibility in thinking, fostering creativity and problem-solving skills. Moreover, mindfulness promotes metacognition, the awareness and regulation of one's own thinking processes, enabling individuals to become more effective learners.

Because racial discrimination cuts people's trust in each other, mindfulness cultivates qualities such as empathy, compassion, and non-judgmental acceptance, which are vital for positive interpersonal relationships. By enhancing self-awareness and emotional regulation, it enables individuals to respond rather than react to conflicts or stressful situations. Mindfulness also promotes active listening skills and the ability to be fully present with others, fostering more harmonious and empathetic relationships.

TRANSFORMING TO RACIAL INCLUSION

Identifying racism is only the first step toward addressing it effectively. It necessitates raising awareness, fostering empathy, and engaging in meaningful conversations. By actively seeking knowledge and understanding, individuals can identify their own biases and work toward dismantling them. Racial healing is the second step toward racial inclusion. With racial healing, BIPOC and White people are ready to create a new world with racial inclusion.

Engaging with diverse voices, supporting anti-racist initiatives, and advocating for equitable policies are crucial steps toward combating racism in all its forms. This chapter will explore the application of (a) openness to diversity, (b) empathy across cultures, (c) celebration of culture-specific strengths, and (d) anti-racism pedagogy to transform racial inclusion.

Openness to Diversity

To create racial inclusion, it is essential for individuals to develop intercultural competence and embrace diversity. The recognition and understanding of both similarities and differences among individuals can foster a more inclusive and harmonious society. As racial inclusion enhances interconnectedness between individuals and nations, fostering openness to diversity is crucial for societal development, individual growth, and the overall well-being of communities.

Openness to diversity starts with self-acceptance and self-reflection on who we are and enables us to identify our own biases and preferences when it comes to universality and diversity. This heightened self-awareness serves as a foundation for personal growth, allowing individuals to challenge their viewpoints and expand their cultural knowledge. Such self-awareness, in fact, turns into self-confidence. For BIPOC individuals, openness to diversity expands the horizons of their worldview while expediting their racial healing.

Besides, openness to diversity helps people to learn to welcome others from different racial/ethnic backgrounds and create culturally responsive strategies that incorporate diverse perspectives. Because openness to diversity helps White people reduce the discomfort, denial, and defensiveness when they are involved in conversations regarding race-related issues, such openness will encourage them to engage with all people regardless of their backgrounds. Openness to diversity expedites racial inclusion by enriching cultural exchanges and exposing individuals to different traditions, beliefs, languages, and artistic expressions. Such encounters foster mutual respect, appreciation, and intercultural dialogue, ultimately contributing to the preservation and promotion of global cultural heritage.

Importantly, openness to diversity promotes social justice and involves everyone, including White people. Emphasizing the role of openness to diversity in maintaining White people's empathy is essential. Diversity programs should integrate openness to diversity with the racial identity of BIPOC and White people to create a more inclusive climate. Additionally, intercultural programs and workshops can be conducted to create dialogues between White people and BIPOC who experience racism. These programs can help White people understand the impact of racism and reflect on their own privileges.

Another reason openness to diversity is critical for racial inclusion is that it enhances creativity and innovation as it brings together individuals with diverse perspectives, experiences, and backgrounds. This diversity of thought fosters the development of unique solutions to complex problems and encourages innovation in various fields, such as scientific research, technology, and business. Being together across races and ethnicities promotes social cohesion and reduces the likelihood of conflict by fostering understanding and empathy among individuals from different backgrounds. It allows for the forming social networks and collaborative relationships across diverse communities, breaking down stereotypes and prejudices.

Openness to diversity is crucial for the progress and well-being of contemporary society. Embracing diversity promotes creativity, social cohesion and enriches cultural exchange. In education, creating inclusive learning environments, embracing diversity, and promoting intercultural competence are essential to preparing people for a world characterized by diversity and interconnectivity. It is necessary for educational institutions to adopt strategies that foster inclusivity, such as promoting staff and student diversity, implementing anti-bias education, and encouraging collaborative activities. By promoting openness to diversity, we can create a more just and compassionate world where everyone is valued and their unique contributions are recognized and celebrated.

Because racial inclusion is based on welcoming every person and each unique and different perspective, when exposed to diverse perspectives, people with an openness to diversity can learn to cultivate critical thinking and perspective-taking skills. It enables them to understand complex societal issues from different angles and develop a nuanced understanding of the world, preparing them to be active and engaged citizens. Such perspective-taking skills in racial inclusion can also promote intercultural competence, enabling BIPOC and White people to communicate effectively, collaborate, and negotiate across cultures, preparing them for diverse workplaces and international settings.

Empathy across Cultures

Empathy is the ability to understand and share the feelings of others, walk in their shoes, and experience the world from their point of view. It is a fundamental aspect of human interaction and has significant implications for personal relationships, social harmony, and intercultural understanding. While empathy is a universal human trait, its manifestation and expression may vary across cultures due to the influence of cultural norms, values, and socialization processes. With empathy across cultures, people can appreciate the similarities and differences between cultures and demonstrate sincere and genuine care that fits with others' cultural contexts.

Racial inclusion plays a crucial role in shaping how empathy is perceived, communicated, and practiced across different societies. For instance, collectivist cultures, such as those found in many Asian countries, often emphasize the importance of harmony, interdependence, and collective well-being. In such cultures, empathy may be directed toward maintaining social relationships, preserving group cohesion, and prioritizing the needs of the community over individual desires. On the other hand, individualistic cultures, like those prevalent in Western societies, tend to prioritize individual freedom, autonomy, and self-expression. Consequently, empathy may be more directed toward the protection of individual rights, personal growth, and the pursuit of happiness.

Furthermore, racial inclusion can also be observed in the display of empathy. In some cultures, emotional restraint and self-control are considered essential, leading individuals to suppress or conceal their empathetic responses in public settings. This is particularly prevalent in countries influenced by Confucian values, where maintaining composure and avoiding the display of excessive emotions are highly valued. Conversely, cultures that encourage emotional expressiveness and direct communication may exhibit a more pronounced empathetic response, such as crying, hugging, or physical contact. These cultural differences in displaying empathy highlight the importance of understanding and respecting diverse cultural practices when engaging in cross-cultural interactions.

Respecting everyone's culture and racial inclusion puts empathy in the context of cultural variations. First and foremost, cultural norms and values shape individuals' understanding of empathy and its role within society. For example, empathy may be viewed as a social obligation in cultures that prioritize interdependence, while in individualistic cultures, it may be considered a personal choice. Additionally, the overall level of economic development and societal well-being can influence the manifestation of empathy within a culture. When societies face economic hardships or political instability, empathy may be directed toward immediate needs and survival, making it more challenging to exhibit empathy toward distant or unrelated individuals.

Thus, empathy across cultures is crucial for fostering intercultural understanding, reducing cultural biases, and promoting effective communication and collaboration. By recognizing that different cultures may express empathy in diverse ways, individuals can navigate cross-cultural interactions with increased sensitivity and respect. Developing cross-cultural empathy involves suspending judgment, actively listening to others' experiences, and recognizing the contextual factors that shape individual perceptions and actions. This ability to empathize across cultures allows for a deeper appreciation of cultural diversity, nurturing positive and meaningful relationships in an increasingly globalized world.

Self-empathy: Acceptance of Discomfort

Empathy is a powerful tool for showing care to other people. It is also an important skill for fostering self-acceptance. When people apply empathy to show care to others, they can also use empathy to empower themselves to accept their discomfort. For White people, empathy could be a critical tool for empowering themselves to accept their discomfort about race-related issues.

Thus, White people's self-empathy can help them build acceptance for their discomfort. It is uncomfortable to consider one's racism and involvement in racist systems, and we have argued that White people will often prioritize their comfort during such moments, using strategies characterized by disengagement and avoidance, even though these strategies are likely to perpetuate longer-term harm. Rather than trying to avoid one's emotions, self-empathy helps White people to accept their emotions. Self-empathy helps White people understand that it takes more courage to accept rather than avoid their discomfort.

Self-empathy involves an intention to recognize people's efforts to acknowledge the emotion and discomfort they have. Self-empathy also helps White people to be aware of their negative emotions without judgment or blaming. In doing so, White people can recognize that their negative emotional reactions toward race-related issues are typical responses when they are in stressful situations. Indeed, engaging in a race-related conversation that they might have had no experience with before could be stressful. Self-empathy can also help White people avoid negative emotional reactions to their own emotions (e.g., feeling fatigued about feeling guilty), which can be particularly damaging. Self-empathy can facilitate White people's capacity to accept the negative emotions of Black community members experiencing racism. Self-empathy also allows White people to develop and express their reactions and discomfort instead of avoiding expressing their feelings.

Celebrate Culture-specific Strengths

Recognizing and celebrating each culture's specific strengths promote racial inclusion.

Culture plays a significant role in shaping individuals and societies around the world. It encompasses beliefs, values, traditions, and practices that are passed down from one generation to another. Every culture is unique and possesses its own set of strengths and assets that contribute to the overall well-being of its members. Recognizing and harnessing these culture-specific strengths is crucial, especially in the field of education.

Culture-specific strengths refer to the positive attributes embedded within a culture that contribute to the individual and collective growth of its members. These strengths are often based on culturally grounded ideologies, practices, and values. When these strengths are recognized and utilized, they can enhance educational outcomes, promoting academic success, personal growth, and socio-emotional development among people.

The Strengths of Black Culture

Black culture, also referred to as African American culture, is a vibrant amalgamation of customs, traditions, beliefs, art forms, and social norms that have evolved from the historical experiences of African Americans in the United States. Throughout history, Black culture has demonstrated an extraordinary capacity to adapt, preserve, and create. It is crucial to explore the strengths of Black culture and how they have shaped the community's identity, overcome adversity, and contributed to society's transformation. Black culture draws its strength from the indomitable spirit of resilience that has been forged through centuries of hardship and oppression. African Americans endured the brutality of the transatlantic slave trade, centuries of enslavement, segregation, and ongoing racial discrimination. Despite these adversities, Black culture has remained resilient, showcasing a remarkable ability to sustain and flourish under challenging circumstances.

One of the notable strengths of Black culture is its emphasis on the importance of community. From the days of slavery, where families and communities were often separated, to the civil rights movement and beyond, African Americans have fostered a sense of collective identity and support. This emphasis on community resilience has contributed to preserving traditions, values, and social structures within Black culture.

Black culture boasts a rich artistic heritage that has dramatically influenced various art forms, including literature, music, dance, and visual arts. These artistic expressions have been significant for their aesthetic allure and have served as powerful tools for social commentary, empowerment, and cultural preservation. African American literature, for instance, has been instrumental in shedding light on the African American experience, delving into themes of identity, racism, and societal transformation. Works like Ralph Ellison's "Invisible Man," Maya Angelou's "I Know Why the Caged Bird Sings," and Toni Morrison's "Beloved" vividly capture the struggles and triumphs of African Americans, offering a platform for their voices to be heard.

Music, an integral part of Black culture, has given birth to diverse genres such as jazz, blues, gospel, hip-hop, and R&B. These forms of music have not only entertained but have also served as conduits for social and political activism. Artists such as Nina Simone, Bob Marley, Public Enemy, and Kendrick Lamar have used their music to reflect the realities of the Black community, advocate for justice, and inspire change.

The strengths of Black culture are further evidenced in the resurgence of cultural pride and identity among African Americans. Despite centuries of marginalization and the erasure of Black history and achievements in mainstream narratives, the Black community has found ways to reclaim its heritage and celebrate its contributions to society. Black history and cultural celebrations, such as Black History Month and Juneteenth, have gained prominence in recent years, providing opportunities for the wider society not only to learn about the accomplishments of African Americans but also to appreciate and honor their ongoing contributions. This resurgence of cultural pride has positively impacted the self-esteem, mental well-being, and collective consciousness of African Americans, allowing them to redefine and shape their own narrative.

With Black culture's strength, resilience, and creativity that have endured through centuries of adversity, Black pioneers led the civil rights movement, Black Lives Matter, and other critical movements, and Black people enriched this country. Its capacity to adapt, preserve traditions, and innovate within various spheres of society has made an indelible mark on the cultural landscape of the United States. Acknowledging these strengths can foster a deeper appreciation and understanding of African American experiences while also providing a roadmap for our collective progress toward justice, equality, and racial inclusion.

The Strengths of Asian Culture

Asian culture is rich and diverse, encompassing numerous ethnic groups, languages, traditions, and philosophies. With a history spanning thousands of years, Asian cultures have developed unique strengths and values, enabling them to thrive and overcome challenges. It is critical to explore the various strengths of Asian culture, including its emphasis on family and community, respect for elders and authority, holistic approach to health and wellness, disciplined work ethic, and resilience in the face of adversity. These strengths not only contribute to the cultural fabric of Asian societies but also offer valuable lessons for individuals and communities around the world.

Asian cultures place significant importance on the concept of f*amily and community*. Family is considered the primary unit of society, and filial piety, or respect for one's parents and elders, is deeply ingrained in Asian value systems. This strength contributes to the close-knit nature of Asian communities, fostering a sense of belonging, support, and collective responsibility. Strong family bonds provide a support system during challenging times and promote intergenerational knowledge transfer and value preservation.

Respect for elders and authority is another core strength of Asian cultures. Elders are regarded as a source of wisdom and guidance, and their opinions hold great weight in decision-making processes. This respect extends to teachers, leaders, and authority figures in various spheres of life, reflecting a deep-rooted focus on hierarchy and discipline. By valuing the wisdom of older generations and respecting those in positions of authority, Asian cultures promote a sense of order, stability, and harmonious social relationships.

Asian cultures have long emphasized a *holistic approach to health and wellness*. Traditional healing practices such as Traditional Chinese Medicine (TCM), Ayurveda, and acupuncture highlight the interconnectedness of the mind, body, and spirit. These ancient practices prioritize prevention, balance, and natural remedies, recognizing that individual well-being is intricately linked to environmental and social factors. By addressing health holistically, Asian cultures promote a broader perspective on well-being and offer valuable insights into self-care practices and the importance of preventive measures.

Asian cultures are renowned for their disciplined and diligent *work ethic*. Cultivated through the influence of Confucianism and other philosophical traditions, this strength promotes perseverance, dedication, and a commitment to excellence. In Asian societies, hard work and education are highly valued, with an emphasis on striving for personal and collective progress. This work ethic has led to remarkable advancements in various fields, including technology, science, and business, and continues to fuel economic growth and success in Asia.

Asian cultures have a long history of *resilience in the face of adversity*. Whether it be natural disasters, wars, or economic crises, Asian societies have demonstrated remarkable strength and adaptability. This strength is often rooted in deeply embedded values such as perseverance, humility, and a focus on long-term goals. Through resilience, Asian cultures have bounced back from setbacks, rebuilt communities, and forged ahead, showcasing the power of collective effort and determination.

The Strengths of Latino/a Culture

Latino/a culture refers to the communal values, traditions, and heritage of individuals with Latin American roots. The rich tapestry of Latino/a culture has many strengths that shape the lives of individuals within this community. Exploring these strengths allows us to appreciate and celebrate the resilience, unity, and diversity that define Latino/a culture. It is critical to highlight these strengths and emphasize their significance within Latino/a communities, ultimately shedding light on the importance of embracing diversity in education and society at large.

One of the most prominent strengths of Latino/a culture is resilience. Latino/a communities have faced numerous challenges and adversities throughout history, including migration, discrimination, and socioeconomic disparities. However, through their resilience, members of these communities have shown remarkable strength and adaptability. This resilience stems from their cultural values, such as family, faith, and community support. These values have enabled Latinos/as to overcome obstacles and persistently pursue their dreams, often against all odds. This resilience is a vital strength that can teach us all the importance of determination and perseverance.

Another exceptional strength of the Latino/a culture is its emphasis on unity and solidarity. Latinos/as highly value their families and communities, fostering a strong sense of belonging and interconnectedness. The concept of "familismo" plays a crucial role in maintaining family bonds and a collective identity. This unity extends beyond immediate family members to include extended relatives, neighbors, and close friends. As a result, Latino/a culture promotes a deep sense of support, trust, and cooperation among its members. This unity acts as a vital force in facing shared challenges and advocating for the rights and well-being of the community as a whole.

Latino/a culture encompasses a wide range of countries, ethnicities, and linguistic backgrounds. Embracing this diversity, the Latino/a community thrives on the rich blend of customs, traditions, and languages that contribute to its cultural mosaic. From Peru to Puerto Rico and Mexico to the Dominican Republic, each country brings its unique cultural expressions, food, music, and art. This diversity is a tremendous strength, fostering a deep appreciation for multiculturalism and the importance of inclusivity. By recognizing the value of diversity within Latino/a culture, we can learn valuable lessons about tolerance, cultural exchange, and the celebration of differences.

Understanding and appreciating the strengths of Latino/a culture is essential within an educational context. Schools should incorporate culturally responsive pedagogical practices that honor and reflect the experiences and heritage of Latino/a people. By doing so, educators can create inclusive learning environments that validate the cultural identities of these people and increase their engagement and success. Furthermore, Latino/a culture's emphasis on resilience, unity, and diversity can be powerful examples to inspire all people to overcome obstacles, foster collaboration, and embrace diversity within their classrooms and in broader society.

The strengths of Latino/a culture, including resilience, unity, and cultural diversity, are fundamental to understanding and appreciating the experiences and contributions of the Latino/a community. Through their resilience in the face of adversity, unity within their families and communities, and celebration of cultural diversity, Latinos/as exemplify the values that empower individuals and strengthen communities. Racial inclusion recognizes and embraces these strengths; society can learn from the Latino/a community's experiences and move toward a more inclusive and equitable future.

The Strengths of American Indian Culture

American Indian culture encompasses a rich and diverse range of traditions, customs, beliefs, and practices that have been passed down through generations. One of the significant strengths of American Indian culture is its resilience. Throughout history, American Indians have faced immense challenges such as colonization, forced assimilation, displacement, and discrimination. Despite these adversities, their culture has managed to survive and thrive. This resilience can be attributed to their strong sense of identity, inherent spirituality, and the preservation of traditional knowledge.

American Indians deeply understand and are proud of their identity based on their unique cultural heritage. They honor their ancestors, their land, and their customs, which help to reinforce their sense of self-worth and resilience in the face of adversity. This strong cultural identity has played a vital role in empowering individuals and communities with a sense of purpose, helping them to navigate the challenges they have encountered throughout history.

Additionally, American Indian culture is deeply rooted in spirituality. Many traditional ceremonies and practices are centered around connecting with the spiritual world and seeking guidance and strength from higher powers. This spiritual connection has provided comfort and resilience for many American Indians, giving them hope and guidance during difficult times.

Furthermore, preserving traditional knowledge within American Indian communities has been vital in maintaining their cultural resilience. Elders play a crucial role in passing down oral traditions, stories, and rituals to younger generations, ensuring these practices remain alive. This passing down of knowledge not only strengthens the cultural fabric but also equips younger generations with the tools to face contemporary challenges while drawing upon the wisdom of their ancestors.

Another strength of American Indian culture is its deep interconnectedness with nature. American Indians view the environment as a living entity that deserves respect and protection. Traditional ecological knowledge, which encompasses a deep understanding of the natural world, has been passed down through generations, guiding sustainable practices and harmony with nature. The concept of "Mother Earth" is prevalent in American Indian culture, highlighting the belief that we are all connected to and dependent on the earth for our survival. This perspective fosters a sense of responsibility and stewardship toward the environment. American Indians view themselves as caretakers of the land and strive to live in harmony with nature, taking only what is necessary and giving back to ensure the sustainable use of resources.

This interconnectedness with nature is beneficial for ecological preservation and nurtures a sense of balance and well-being in individuals and communities. Spending time in natural surroundings, whether through rituals, ceremonies, or daily activities, is believed to restore and maintain physical, emotional, and spiritual health.

American Indian culture strongly emphasizes community and collective well-being. Traditionally, American Indian societies were organized around kinship bonds, extended families, and tribal affiliations. This communal structure provided a support network and shared responsibility and decision-making.

Community gatherings, ceremonies, and rituals are essential aspects of American Indian culture, fostering a sense of belonging and unity. These events create opportunities for individuals to come together, share experiences, exchange knowledge, and strengthen social bonds. They also provide a platform for resolving conflicts and addressing challenges collectively.

American Indian culture promotes inclusivity and egalitarianism, valuing the contributions and perspectives of all community members. Leadership within American Indian cultures is often based on skills, wisdom, and generosity rather than hierarchical structures. This inclusive approach encourages collaboration and cooperation, enabling the community as a whole to thrive.

The Strengths of White Culture

Although some people believe that White culture relates to Whiteness, White culture may still play a role in shaping US society, influencing worldviews, and defining identities. White culture, as a result of historical, geographical, and sociopolitical factors, has evolved, giving rise to a diverse range of strengths that have contributed to the development and progress of societies.

To fully comprehend the strengths of White culture, it is necessary to consider the historical context that has shaped it. The scientific, artistic, and technological achievements of ancient European civilizations laid the foundations for advancements in various fields. White culture's ability to preserve and disseminate knowledge through the Renaissance, Enlightenment, and Industrial Revolution epochs bears testament to its strength and adaptability.

White culture has made significant intellectual contributions across various disciplines, including philosophy, art, science, and literature. The ancient Greeks, for instance, pioneered philosophy and democracy, establishing a legacy that continues to shape modern political systems. The Renaissance period witnessed an explosion of intellectual endeavors, with White figures like Leonardo da Vinci and Michelangelo revolutionizing art and pushing the boundaries of human creativity. Additionally, White scientists and inventors, such as Isaac Newton, Thomas Edison, and Marie Curie, have made groundbreaking discoveries that continue to shape the world we live in today.

White culture has consistently produced innovative advancements in technology, benefiting societies worldwide. From the invention of the printing press by Johannes Gutenberg to the industrial and digital revolutions, White culture's contributions have transformed economies and societies alike. This technological prowess has paved the way for advancements in fields such as medicine, transportation, communication, and information technology, thereby improving the quality of life for countless individuals globally.

The strengths of White culture lie in its legacy of intellectual curiosity, artistic expression, scientific discovery, and technological progress. However, it is crucial to acknowledge that celebrating the strengths of White culture should not be done at the expense of devaluing or overlooking the contributions of other diverse cultures. The recognition of the strengths of White culture does not justify or normalize the racism related to White supremacy, White privilege, and other racism-related concepts of Whiteness. Also, the celebration of the strengths in White culture cannot replace or dismiss the discomfort, defensiveness, or denial when some White people discuss race-related topics.

Anti-racism Pedagogy

Education is a fundamental pillar of society and plays a crucial role in shaping individuals' beliefs, attitudes, and actions. However, education systems worldwide have historically perpetuated inequality, discrimination, and racism. As a result, anti-racism pedagogy has emerged as an essential approach to transform education and promote equity, diversity, and social justice. Anti-racism pedagogy is a transformative educational framework that identifies, analyzes, and challenges institutionalized and systemic racism in educational settings. It seeks to provide people with the knowledge, skills, and attitudes necessary to understand, confront, and dismantle racism. Anti-racist educators actively work toward creating inclusive classrooms, promoting multicultural perspectives, and nurturing critical consciousness in people to combat racism at an individual and systemic level. Anti-racism pedagogy plays a crucial role in racial inclusion.

Fostering Racial Inclusiveness

Anti-racism pedagogy ensures that all people, regardless of their racial or ethnic background, feel included and valued in the education system. By recognizing and challenging racist beliefs and practices, teachers can create an environment that respects and embraces diversity, fostering a sense of belonging for every student.

Promoting Critical Thinking

Anti-racism pedagogy encourages critical thinking and analysis of societal power structures, privilege, and oppression. Through open discussions, collaborative learning, and the exploration of diverse perspectives, people can develop a deeper understanding of racism and develop skills to challenge it effectively. To make the voice of critical thinking louder, it is necessary to utilize counternarratives and counter-texts, an effective strategy for challenging dominant narratives perpetuating racism. By presenting alternative viewpoints and narratives, teachers can help people critically analyze and deconstruct biased interpretations and develop a more nuanced understanding of societal issues.

Empowering Marginalized Communities

Anti-racism pedagogy empowers marginalized communities by providing them with a platform to voice their experiences, challenges, and aspirations. It acknowledges their lived realities and seeks to rectify the historical and systemic injustices they face in education and society. Moreover, anti-racist educators actively work to create a safe space where people can share their stories without judgment or prejudice. To further empower underrepresented or marginalized groups, an effective anti-racism classroom incorporates diverse perspectives in the curriculum, ensuring representation and highlighting contributions from marginalized communities. This may involve integrating multicultural literature, historical narratives, and contemporary case studies that promote critical thinking and foster empathy.

Building Cultural Competence

Cultural competence is a foundation for racial inclusion. Anti-racism pedagogy emphasizes the need for culturally responsive teaching practices. By incorporating diverse cultural perspectives, histories, and experiences into the curriculum, educators can enhance people's cultural competence, empathy, and understanding. This approach prepares people to navigate and engage with the complexities of a multicultural society.

Challenging Biases and Stereotypes

Anti-racism pedagogy challenges racial biases and stereotypes that perpetuate discrimination and racism. By exposing people to counternarratives and providing accurate historical context, teachers can mitigate the harmful effects of societal stereotypes and facilitate more informed and inclusive conversations about race.

Without challenging biases and stereotypes, it is almost impossible to build racial inclusion. To empower people to challenge biases and stereotypes, open discussions, debates, and dialogues around race-related topics are essential strategies for an anti-racism classroom. This approach allows people to critically examine their biases and prejudices, challenge stereotypes, and develop informed opinions. Teachers play a crucial role in facilitating these conversations through active listening, providing safe spaces, and guiding productive discussions.

Empowering Active Citizenry

Anti-racist education empowers people to become agents of change in their communities. By equipping them with critical consciousness, empathy, and advocacy skills, anti-racism pedagogy fosters active citizenship and encourages people to challenge racism beyond the classroom walls.

Reducing Racial Achievement Gaps

Research shows that anti-racist education can help reduce racial achievement gaps by addressing the systemic barriers that hinder the success of marginalized people. By identifying and dismantling racist policies, practices, and curricula, anti-racist educators work toward creating an equitable educational environment that ensures equal opportunities for all people.

Chapter 4

Racial Inclusion

Benefits to All People

Racial inclusion is not only a moral imperative but also brings numerous benefits to individuals, communities, and societies. Moreover, racial inclusion benefits *all people*, and *everyone* deserves to receive and experience positive outcomes. Racial inclusion also sets up a positive example that the benefits will be shared equally. When individuals from different racial backgrounds are valued and included, they can fully contribute their talents, expertise, and perspectives. By tapping into diverse individuals' collective knowledge and experiences, societies can foster innovation, creativity, and problem-solving, leading to more robust economic growth and enhanced social cohesion.

PRINCIPLES OF RACIAL INCLUSION

The principles of racial inclusion create positive outcomes for all people. Racial inclusion promotes social justice and reduces socioeconomic disparities. It creates a society where everyone has equitable access to opportunities, resources, and social services. This, in turn, reduces the prevalence of poverty, crime rates, and social unrest. Racially inclusive societies also experience improved mental and physical health outcomes, as individuals feel a sense of belonging, safety, and support.

Racial inclusion refers to the practice of ensuring that people of all races and ethnicities are treated fairly and respectfully and have equal access to opportunities, resources, and benefits within a particular community, organization, or society. It is crucial to promoting diversity, equity, and social justice. Fundamental principles and practices associated with racial inclusion include:

First, racial inclusion focuses on equal opportunities. Racial inclusion involves equal opportunities for individuals of all races to participate and succeed in various aspects of life, such as education, employment, and civic engagement.

Second, racial inclusion can only be effective with representation. It is critical to ensure diverse representation at all levels of an organization or in decision-making processes, which is crucial for racial inclusion. This includes representation in leadership positions, on boards, and in other influential roles.

Third, cultural competence is another indispensable principle of racial inclusion. Embracing and understanding diverse cultures are essential for fostering racial inclusion. This involves recognizing and respecting different cultural norms, practices, and perspectives.

Fourth, non-discrimination is a critical component of racial inclusion. Racial inclusion requires the prohibition of discriminatory practices and policies based on race. This includes addressing implicit biases that may contribute to unequal treatment.

Fifth, racial inclusion includes equitable policies for people from different races. Implementing policies that address historical and systemic inequalities is fundamental to racial inclusion. This may involve affirmative action programs or other measures to correct past and ongoing disparities.

Six, promoting education and awareness about the historical and contemporary issues related to race is crucial for fostering understanding and empathy. This includes recognizing and challenging stereotypes and biases. Also, using inclusive and respectful language for all racial and ethnic groups helps create an environment where everyone feels valued and recognized. Finally, community engagement involving diverse communities in decision-making processes and community initiatives contributes to a more inclusive and equitable society.

Racial inclusion is part of a broader effort to build a more just and equitable world. It acknowledges and seeks to address historical and systemic injustices, working toward creating environments where individuals from all racial backgrounds can thrive and contribute to the fullest extent of their abilities. It is important to note that achieving racial inclusion requires ongoing commitment, awareness, and active efforts to dismantle barriers and promote equality.

POSITIVE OUTCOMES OF RACIAL INCLUSION

Racial inclusion is a critical aspect of society, and its positive outcomes span various areas, including social equality, empathy development, and economic prosperity. It is essential to explore these positive outcomes in detail, providing evidence from research and real-world examples to support these claims. Racial inclusion benefits marginalized communities and enriches society as a whole by fostering understanding and progress.

Equality and Social Cohesion

Racial inclusion is pivotal in creating a more equitable society. By providing equal opportunities and combating discrimination, individuals from all racial backgrounds can actively participate in various spheres of life, such as education, employment, and politics. Inclusive policies and practices enhance social cohesion, dismantling barriers and prejudices that hinder progress. For instance, a study conducted by the Center for Economic and Social Inclusion found that workplaces promoting racial diversity experience higher levels of employee satisfaction and increased productivity.

Empathy and Cultural Appreciation

Racial inclusion facilitates experiential learning, enabling individuals to develop empathy and understanding toward different racial and ethnic backgrounds. Exposure to diverse perspectives cultivates a broader understanding of societal challenges and fosters empathy toward marginalized communities. Schools and educational institutions play a vital role in promoting multicultural education, dismantling stereotypes, and nurturing respect for differences. Research conducted by the American Psychological Association suggests that multicultural education enhances cognitive skills, empathy, and cross-cultural understanding.

Economic Prosperity and Innovation

Racial inclusion has far-reaching economic benefits, contributing to innovation and prosperity. A diverse workforce brings together individuals with varied backgrounds, experiences, and skills, fostering creativity and problem-solving abilities. A study by McKinsey & Company found that companies with racial diversity in their executive teams are 33 percent more likely to outperform their competitors in profitability. Furthermore, inclusion gives rise to entrepreneurship opportunities, as individuals from marginalized communities innovate and contribute to economic growth. California, a state with diverse racial demographics, is often regarded as an economic powerhouse, exemplifying the positive correlation between inclusion and prosperity.

International Reputation and Soft Power

A nation's commitment to racial inclusion enhances its international reputation and soft power. Countries that actively promote diversity and inclusivity are seen as progressive and advanced, attracting talent, tourism, and investment. For example, Canada positions itself as an inclusive country, which has contributed to its reputation as one of the world's most welcoming nations. This positive image enhances economic growth and improves diplomacy and cooperation in global affairs.

Therefore, racial inclusion yields many positive outcomes, promoting social equality, empathy, economic prosperity, and international reputation. Embracing diversity allows for the equal participation of individuals from all racial backgrounds, nurturing an inclusive society where everyone can reach their potential. Society can bridge gaps, dismantle prejudices, and foster understanding through inclusive education, workplaces, and policies. Ultimately, racial inclusion benefits marginalized communities and enriches society as a whole, contributing to a more equitable, empathetic, and prosperous world.

BENEFITS OF RACIAL INCLUSION AT THE INDIVIDUAL LEVEL

Racial inclusion refers to creating an environment that embraces diversity and promotes equal opportunities for individuals of various racial backgrounds. It has numerous benefits at the individual level, emphasizing personal growth, emotional well-being, and increased understanding and empathy toward others. Racial inclusion promotes breaking down social barriers, open-mindedness, and the creation of a harmonious society.

Racial inclusion plays a vital role in individual growth by challenging preconceived notions and biases. Exposure to individuals from diverse racial backgrounds allows people to expand their perspectives, enhancing their critical thinking skills and adaptability. By interacting with people from different racial backgrounds, individuals can develop the ability to see beyond stereotypes and delve into the complexities of human experiences. This growth fosters a sense of self-reflection, promotes self-awareness, and helps individuals redefine their identity within a broader context.

Racial inclusion positively impacts an individual's emotional well-being by cultivating a sense of belonging and reducing feelings of isolation. Feeling included and valued contributes to an individual's self-esteem and overall mental health. By fostering an environment where individuals from all racial backgrounds feel safe and accepted, racial inclusion helps to create a sense of community and mutual respect. This sense of belonging combats negative emotions such as social exclusion, discrimination, and marginalization, increasing happiness and life satisfaction.

Racial inclusion encourages individuals to develop a deeper understanding and empathy toward others. By engaging in meaningful conversations and fostering cross-cultural relationships, individuals gain insights into diverse perspectives, experiences, and challenges different racial communities face. This increased understanding helps eradicate stereotypes and prejudices and promotes tolerance and acceptance. Empathy, in turn, builds bridges between people from various racial backgrounds, fostering a more compassionate and cohesive society.

Racial inclusion breaks down social barriers, overcoming divisions within communities and societies. Racial inclusion promotes social and upward economic mobility for individuals from all racial backgrounds by providing equal opportunities and ensuring fairness in all aspects of life. It challenges systemic barriers that have historically limited the access and opportunities for certain racial groups, leading to a fairer and more equitable society for all.

Racial inclusion encourages open-mindedness, which sparks creativity, innovation, and collaboration. New and unique solutions are discovered by fostering an environment where individuals feel comfortable expressing their perspectives and ideas, regardless of their racial background. Diverse teams and workplaces thrive on exchanging ideas, creativity, and different ways of thinking that can only be achieved through racial inclusion.

Taken together, racial inclusion at the individual level brings numerous benefits, including personal growth, emotional well-being, increased understanding and empathy, breaking down social barriers, and fostering open-mindedness and innovation. It is a powerful practice that contributes to the creation of a harmonious, equal, and compassionate society. As individuals embrace racial inclusion, they are enriched by the diversity around them, allowing for continuous growth and a more inclusive, interconnected world.

Racial Inclusion Is a Collective Healing

Racial inclusion serves as a collective healing process for individuals and communities. By examining its impact on education and employment systems, social cohesion, and individual well-being, this chapter aims to highlight its importance as a catalyst for societal transformation.

By embracing diversity within educational institutions, students have the opportunity to learn from different perspectives, cultures, and experiences, fostering empathy, cultural understanding, and social togetherness. Furthermore, inclusive education systems empower individuals from marginalized racial communities by providing access to resources and opportunities that were previously denied to them, thus addressing historical injustices and contributing to the collective healing process.

Racial inclusion plays a fundamental role in fostering social connections within communities. By acknowledging and embracing racial diversity, societies can bridge racial divisions and create meaningful dialogue and interaction spaces. Inclusive communities encourage collaboration among individuals from different racial backgrounds, strengthening social bonds and collective healing. Engaging in open conversations about racial issues, sharing experiences, and acknowledging systemic racism contributes to the dismantling of racial barriers and lays the foundation for transformative social change.

Moreover, racial inclusion promotes social justice and equality by challenging the unequal power dynamics that marginalize racial communities. By creating inclusive policies and frameworks, institutions and governments can address structural and systemic racism, fostering a sense of belonging and unity among diverse populations. This collective healing process benefits marginalized racial communities and leads to a more harmonious and equitable society for all.

Racial inclusion profoundly impacts the well-being of individuals from marginalized racial communities. Individuals develop a stronger sense of self-worth and identity by experiencing inclusion and representation in various aspects of life, such as media, politics, and community organizations. This sense of belonging enhances their mental and emotional well-being, empowering them to challenge racial stereotypes and achieve their full potential.

Furthermore, racial inclusion provides individuals with opportunities for personal growth and advancement, breaking the cycle of socioeconomic disparities associated with racial discrimination. By leveling the playing field and providing equal access to education, healthcare, and resources, racial inclusion enables individuals to overcome systemic barriers and improve their quality of life. This uplifts their well-being and contributes to the collective healing process by addressing the long-standing effects of racial injustice.

Psychological Benefits

The concept of racial inclusion has gained significant importance in recent years as societies worldwide strive to create a harmonious and equitable environment for all individuals, resulting in numerous psychological benefits.

Enhanced Sense of Belonging. Racial inclusion fosters a sense of belonging and unity among individuals from different racial backgrounds. By welcoming diverse perspectives, cultures, and experiences, society creates an environment where individuals feel appreciated, accepted, and valued. This sense of belonging enhances psychological well-being as it alleviates feelings of alienation and exclusion that individuals of marginalized racial groups may experience. Research has consistently shown that belongingness is a fundamental human need closely linked to mental health outcomes. A study conducted by Baumeister and Leary (1995) revealed that individuals with a strong sense of belonging have higher self-esteem, experience lower levels of anxiety and depression, and are better able to cope with stress. Racial inclusion, therefore, can positively impact an individual's self-perception and overall psychological well-being.

Increased Empathy and Perspective-Taking Abilities. Racial inclusion allows individuals to interact with people from diverse racial backgrounds, fostering empathy and understanding. Regular exposure to different cultures and perspectives can broaden one's worldview and challenge preconceived biases, leading to an increased ability to consider and empathize with the experiences and struggles of individuals from other racial groups. Numerous studies have shown a direct correlation between empathy and psychological well-being related to racial inclusion. Empathy promotes prosocial behavior, reduces prejudice, and enhances social connections, all contributing to improved mental health outcomes. By promoting racial inclusion, society encourages the development of empathy and perspective-taking abilities, leading to more compassionate and supportive relationships among individuals from various racial backgrounds.

Boosting Cognitive Abilities. Racial inclusion has been linked to enhanced cognitive abilities such as creativity, problem-solving, critical thinking, and innovation. Research suggests that diverse teams, where individuals from different racial backgrounds collaborate, tend to analyze problems from various angles and offer unique perspectives, leading to more effective and innovative solutions. A study by Page (2007) revealed that diverse groups outperformed homogeneous groups in tasks requiring problem-solving and creativity. By incorporating individuals from diverse racial backgrounds into workplaces, educational institutions, and communities, society can tap into a rich talent pool and benefit from the cognitive advantages of racial inclusion.

Resilience and Multicultural Competence. Racial inclusion fosters resilience and multicultural competence and makes critical attributes in an increasingly diverse society. By interacting with individuals from different racial backgrounds, individuals develop the ability to adapt to new circumstances, overcome challenges, and thrive in diverse environments. This enhances psychological well-being as individuals become more equipped to handle the complexities of an interconnected and multicultural world. Moreover, multicultural competence allows individuals to navigate intercultural interactions with sensitivity and respect. By understanding and appreciating different cultures, individuals become more culturally sensitive and aware, reducing prejudice and discrimination. This, in turn, fosters social harmony and psychological well-being, as individuals feel valued and respected for their unique identities.

In sum, racial inclusion holds numerous psychological benefits, contributing to individual well-being, social cohesion, and overall mental health. It fosters a sense of belonging, enhances empathy and perspective-taking abilities, boosts cognitive abilities, and promotes resilience and multicultural competence. By prioritizing racial inclusion, societies can create an equitable and harmonious environment that celebrates diversity and values the contributions of individuals from various racial backgrounds. Therefore, institutions, organizations, and policymakers must recognize the significance of racial inclusion and work toward creating inclusive spaces for all individuals in order to reap the psychological benefits it offers.

Emotional Benefits

Racial inclusion and its associated benefits are of immense importance, especially in today's diverse and interconnected society. While the focus on racial inclusion often revolves around practical and societal advantages, such as economic growth and political harmony, an equally valuable aspect lies in the emotional benefits it fosters.

Enhanced Sense of Belonging and Identity. One of the primary emotional benefits of racial inclusion is the enhanced sense of belonging and identity it engenders among individuals. When people from diverse racial backgrounds are included and valued within a community, they are more likely to develop a positive sense of self and a stronger connection to their society. This sense of belonging serves as an emotional anchor, instilling in individuals a feeling of acceptance and validation, ultimately contributing to their overall well-being.

Empathy and Emotional Intelligence Development. Racial inclusion expands exposure to different cultures, perspectives, and experiences. Individuals interacting and engaging with people from diverse racial backgrounds are more likely to cultivate empathy and develop emotional intelligence. Empathizing with someone from a different racial background nurtures compassion, understanding, and open-mindedness. These qualities are essential for personal growth and promoting empathy-based relationships in society, ultimately fostering emotional well-being for individuals and creating a more inclusive society.

Reduced Emotional Stress and Anxiety. Exclusion and marginalization based on race are deeply distressing for those affected. Conversely, racial inclusion functions as a therapeutic intervention, significantly reducing emotional stress and anxiety among individuals. When individuals are included and embraced within diverse communities, they feel safer, more supported, and less burdened by the fear of discrimination. This reduction in emotional stress can transform an individual's mental health, leading to improved overall well-being.

Building Harmonious Community Relations. Racial inclusion catalyzes building harmonious community relations. When individuals from different racial backgrounds are included and valued within a community, it nurtures a sense of unity, belonging, and shared purpose. Inclusive communities are characterized by improved intergroup relations, reduced prejudices, and strengthened social bonds. Such communities create an emotionally supportive and nurturing environment that benefits all their members, fostering a collective sense of healing and harmony.

BENEFITS OF RACIAL INCLUSION AT THE INSTITUTIONAL LEVEL

In recent years, there has been a growing recognition of the importance of racial inclusion at various societal levels. Institutions, such as educational and academic institutions, play a crucial role in shaping societal norms and values. Therefore, actively promoting racial inclusion within these institutions is a moral imperative and a means to foster a more equitable and just society. It is time to delve into the benefits of racial inclusion at the institutional level, focusing on educational institutions and how it positively impacts individuals, communities, and society.

Promoting racial inclusion at the institutional level is critical to achieving equality and social justice. By actively incorporating diversity into institutions, marginalized racial and ethnic groups can thrive and contribute to various fields. This not only helps combat racial discrimination but also challenges stereotypes and systemic biases that perpetuate social inequality. Institutions that prioritize racial inclusion create a fair playing field and send a powerful message that diversity is valued and celebrated.

Racial inclusion in educational institutions leads to improved educational outcomes. Students from diverse racial and ethnic backgrounds bring unique perspectives, experiences, and knowledge into the classroom, enriching the learning environment. Exposure to different cultures and ideas fosters critical thinking, creativity, and empathy among students. Additionally, racially inclusive classrooms promote cross-cultural understanding, reducing racial prejudices and creating a more inclusive society. Research has shown that diverse classrooms enhance students' problem-solving abilities and academic achievement.

Institutional racial inclusion also extends to leadership roles, with diverse representation in decision-making positions. When institutions actively recruit and retain racially diverse staff, faculty, and administrators, it increases the representation of traditionally marginalized groups, inspiring others and fostering an environment of inclusion. Diverse leadership brings diverse perspectives, which ultimately benefit the institution by improving decision-making processes and generating innovative solutions to complex problems.

Employing a racially inclusive approach within institutions fosters innovation and creativity. Diverse teams offer different perspectives on problem-solving and innovative thinking. Organizations with a diverse workforce are more likely to generate novel ideas and attain superior business performance. By embracing racial diversity, institutions can tap into a broader pool of talents, ideas, and experiences, stimulating creativity and pushing the boundaries of knowledge and innovation.

At the institutional level, racial inclusion increases social cohesion and empowers communities. By actively welcoming individuals from diverse backgrounds, institutions create a sense of belonging where everyone feels valued and respected. This promotes positive interpersonal relationships and collaboration among diverse groups, breaking down racial barriers and fostering a more united society. Additionally, racially inclusive institutions support racially and ethnically diverse communities, empowering them to pursue social and economic progress.

Education

Racial inclusion has become an essential aspect of our society in today's ever-diverse world. School education is crucial in promoting racial inclusion by creating an environment that embraces diversity and provides equal opportunities for all students, irrespective of their racial backgrounds. The benefits of racial inclusion in schools and education are manifold and extend far beyond the classroom.

First and foremost, racial inclusion fosters a sense of belonging and acceptance among people. By celebrating and embracing diverse racial identities, schools provide a safe and supportive environment where people feel respected for who they are, regardless of their racial backgrounds. This sense of belonging positively impacts people's mental well-being and overall academic performance.

One of the primary benefits of racial inclusion in education is its positive impact on academic performance. Numerous studies have found that students from diverse racial backgrounds perform better academically when placed in inclusive environments. According to a study conducted by economists at the

University of California, diverse classrooms not only lead to higher academic achievement for minority students but also positively affect the performance of their non-minority peers. This finding was attributed to diverse classrooms exposing all students to different perspectives, challenging their thinking, and improving their problem-solving skills.

Furthermore, racial inclusion in education fosters cultural understanding and empathy among students. When individuals from various racial backgrounds come together in a classroom setting, they can learn from each other's experiences and perspectives. This exposure to diverse cultures and ideas broadens students' horizons and helps them develop a greater appreciation for different cultures. Research conducted by psychologist Beverly Tatum suggests that racial inclusion facilitates the development of cross-cultural skills necessary for individuals to thrive in a diverse society. By interacting with people from different racial backgrounds, students learn to embrace differences, challenge stereotypes, and develop a sense of empathy toward others.

Racial inclusion in education enhances the social fabric of a community, in addition to improving academic performance and cultural understanding. Learning together with students from different racial backgrounds creates a sense of social cohesion and harmony. Research has shown that inclusive education environments foster positive relationships among students, regardless of their racial background, reducing conflict and improving social interactions. Inclusivity also creates a sense of belonging and acceptance, reducing the likelihood of students feeling marginalized or isolated.

Moreover, racial inclusion prepares students for the realities of the modern world and workplace, which are increasingly diverse, and cultural competence is a precious skill. Employers seek individuals who can effectively work and communicate with people from diverse racial backgrounds. Students are better equipped to navigate multicultural environments by fostering racial inclusion in education and promoting a harmonious and inclusive society. In a globalized economy where cultural diversity is the new norm, students who are exposed to various racial backgrounds are better equipped to thrive in diverse workplaces. When interacting with peers from different races, students gain vital interpersonal skills, such as empathy, tolerance, and cultural competence, which are necessary for success in the increasingly interconnected world.

While the benefits of racial inclusion in education are abundant, it is crucial to acknowledge its implementation challenges. Government policies and educational institutions must actively work toward creating inclusive environments that prioritize racial diversity. Educators must receive training on cultural competence, curriculum design, and inclusive teaching practices to ensure all students have equal academic opportunities.

Furthermore, racial inclusion in schools helps break down stereotypes and dispel prejudices. When people from different racial backgrounds collaborate and work together, they challenge existing biases and misconceptions. This leads to a more inclusive society, where individuals are judged based on their character and abilities rather than their racial identity. By dismantling stereotypes, racial inclusion paves the way for a more just and equitable society.

Additionally, racial inclusion in schools promotes multicultural education. By incorporating diverse perspectives, histories, and cultures into the curriculum, schools provide students with a well-rounded education that prepares them to be global citizens. Immersing students in various racial experiences through literature, art, and history fosters a deep understanding and appreciation of different cultures, fostering a spirit of unity amid diversity.

Lastly, racial inclusion in schools contributes to the formation of well-rounded individuals. Exposure to different racial backgrounds prompts students to explore their identities and develop strong self-awareness. When students encounter diverse perspectives and experiences, they are encouraged to critically reflect on their beliefs and values, fostering personal growth and maturity.

Thus, the benefits of racial inclusion in schools are undeniable. By embracing diversity and creating an inclusive environment, schools foster a sense of belonging, prepare students for the real world, challenge stereotypes, promote multicultural education, and contribute to the personal growth of individuals. Schools must prioritize racial inclusion, as it not only shapes the lives of students but also cultivates a more harmonious and equitable society.

Students' cultivation of their understanding and participation in racial inclusion will help them make a more substantial transition to the next step in their learning and career. That is, before being workers and professionals in racial inclusion and social justice, people need to be students with an awareness and appreciation of racial inclusion.

Workplace

Racial inclusion in the workplace is an essential topic in today's globalized world. Racial inclusion creates a welcoming and supportive environment for BIPOC and White people. While progress has been made in terms of racial equality, there is still much work to be done to ensure that individuals from all racial backgrounds are treated fairly and equally in the workplace. When people feel welcomed, respected, and treated fairly, such a positive atmosphere will make them feel safe and appreciated. These positive reactions toward the workplace climate will result in productivity and high contributions to the workplace.

Diversity as a Competitive Advantage. Diversity does not divide people into fragmented small groups. On the opposite, diversity will promote everyone's strengths and unique talents to further contribute to the growth of the workplace. A racially inclusive workplace fosters diversity, which is increasingly recognized as a competitive advantage in various industries. Organizations that embrace diversity tend to attract and retain a broader range of talent, reflecting a diverse customer base and global marketplace. This diversity of perspectives, experiences, and backgrounds leads to better problem-solving and decision-making processes. Companies that value diversity are also more likely to attract a wider range of consumers, as people prefer to engage with inclusive organizations that reflect a more representative society. Ultimately, racial inclusion promotes diversity, allowing organizations to tap into broader skills and perspectives, leading to enhanced performance and competitiveness.

Racial Inclusion Increases Collaboration and Teamwork. Racial inclusion in the workplace helps foster collaboration and teamwork among employees. When individuals from different racial backgrounds come together, they bring diverse ideas, thoughts, and approaches to problem-solving. Organizations can harness the power of collaboration by fostering an inclusive environment that encourages these differences to be openly shared and respected. As individuals learn from one another and work together toward common goals, they develop a deeper understanding and appreciation of diverse perspectives. This, in turn, leads to increased team cohesion, improved communication, and higher levels of employee engagement. Research has shown that teams with higher racial inclusion tend to outperform teams with lower levels of diversity, making collaboration an essential ingredient in organizational success.

Racial Inclusion Promotes Innovation and Creativity. Because racial inclusion values everyone, it can stimulate innovation and creativity. An inclusive environment encourages employees to think outside the box, challenge traditional norms, and propose novel ideas. Organizations are more likely to encounter differing viewpoints and unique insights by bringing together individuals with different racial backgrounds. This interaction facilitates the cross-pollination of ideas, sparking creativity and leading to innovation. Studies have shown that diverse teams generate more innovative solutions and achieve higher performance. By fostering racial inclusion, organizations can tap into their employees' collective knowledge and experiences, enabling them to stay ahead in a rapidly changing and increasingly diverse global economy.

Racial Inclusion Enhances Employee Satisfaction and Retention. Racial inclusion appreciates everyone's contribution. Racial inclusion in the workplace is also vital to enhancing employee satisfaction and retention. When individuals feel valued for who they are, regardless of race, they are more likely to have a positive attitude toward their work. Inclusive workplaces fostering a sense of belonging and respect tend to create a positive work environment, increasing job satisfaction and productivity. Employees are less likely to experience exclusion, discrimination, or marginalization. As a result, they are more motivated, engaged, and committed to their work and the organization. This, in turn, leads to reduced turnover rates and increased retention of top talent, as employees are more likely to stay in an environment where they feel respected and valued.

In sum, racial inclusion is a fundamental aspect of creating a more equitable and just society. Embracing racial inclusion in the workplace is a moral obligation and a strategic imperative for organizations aiming to thrive in a diverse and interconnected world. The benefits of racial inclusion include enhanced diversity, collaboration, innovation, employee satisfaction, and retention. By creating a genuinely inclusive workplace, organizations can capitalize on the power of racial diversity, creating an environment that fosters excellence, creativity, and success.

BENEFITS OF RACIAL INCLUSION AT THE SYSTEMIC LEVEL

Racial inclusion at the systemic level fosters economic growth and innovation by tapping into a wider talent pool and stimulating entrepreneurship. Studies have consistently shown that diverse teams generate better ideas, resulting in higher levels of productivity and innovation. By ensuring equal opportunities for individuals from all racial backgrounds, systemic racial inclusion allows for exploring and utilizing diverse perspectives, ultimately leading to more successful business ventures and economic advancement.

Systemic racial inclusion also enhances problem-solving and decision-making processes. When individuals from various racial backgrounds collaborate in decision-making forums, they bring different experiences, knowledge, and viewpoints to the table. This diversity fosters critical thinking, broadens perspectives, and provides a more comprehensive understanding of complex issues. By encompassing a wider range of voices, systemic racial inclusion facilitates the development of well-rounded policies and solutions to societal problems.

Emphasizing racial inclusion at the systemic level helps build social cohesion and fosters a sense of belonging. When individuals perceive that their unique racial or ethnic identities are respected and embraced, they are more likely to feel connected to society. This increased sense of trust promotes stronger bonds within communities, reduces social tensions, and encourages the formation of robust social networks. By fostering a more cohesive society, systemic racial inclusion ensures that all individuals can participate fully and enjoy a higher quality of life.

Racial inclusion at the systemic level also positively impacts public health outcomes. A study conducted by the World Health Organization revealed that inclusive societies tend to have better overall health indicators, such as lower rates of chronic diseases and increased life expectancy. By reducing disparities in access to healthcare, equalizing opportunities for education and employment, and addressing social determinants of health, systemic racial inclusion contributes to the overall well-being of all individuals, leading to healthier communities.

At its core, racial inclusion at the systemic level acknowledges and addresses historical injustices, creating a more equitable society. This commitment to fairness and equal opportunities aligns with the fundamental principles of democracy, ensuring that all citizens can actively participate in decision-making processes. By dismantling systemic barriers and promoting racial inclusion, societies become more just, democratic, and inclusive for people of all racial backgrounds.

Significantly, racial inclusion reduces disparities. Racial inclusion, which promotes diversity, equity, and equal opportunities, is crucial for reducing such disparities. It is critical to explore the benefits of racial inclusion in education, specifically at the research thesis education level, and to highlight its potential for bridging gaps and promoting equality.

Such a reduction of disparities provides an opportunity to promote positive role models from underrepresented racial groups. By engaging with and showcasing successful researchers from diverse backgrounds, aspiring students are exposed to various role models who can inspire and motivate them. This representation creates a sense of belonging and raises the aspirations of individuals from marginalized racial communities, fostering self-confidence and a belief in their own abilities. As more underrepresented racial groups engage in research and academia, this increased representation contributes to dismantling racial disparities and promotes equality.

COLLABORATION ON ANTI-RACISM

Racism has plagued societies and cultures for centuries, perpetuating prejudices and discrimination based on one's race or ethnicity. With racial inclusion, there has been a growing movement to combat racism and foster inclusivity in various aspects of life. Recognizing the urgency of dismantling systemic racism, collaboration has emerged as a valuable tool in the fight for equality. Racial inclusion highlights the importance of collaboration on anti-racism between people from different racial backgrounds. While numerous strides have been made in acknowledging and addressing deep-rooted systemic issues, it is becoming increasingly evident that collaboration between BIPOC and White people is crucial to effectuate meaningful and lasting change. Racial inclusion highlights the significance of collaboration on anti-racism between BIPOC and White people, emphasizing the importance of understanding, empathy, and shared goals in fostering unity and eradicating racism. As humanity continues its journey toward progress and social harmony, the need for anti-racism measures becomes increasingly crucial. By actively promoting anti-racism, societies can benefit from various positive outcomes, including fostering equality, cultivating empathy, and promoting overall social progress.

The Power of Collaboration

Reflecting on significant historical milestones, such as the Civil Rights Movement and abolitionist movements, collaboration between BIPOC and White activists has proved instrumental in driving progress against racial injustices. Examples like Martin Luther King Jr.'s alliance with White leaders and the Underground Railroad underscore the effectiveness of unity and collaboration. Collaboration between BIPOC and White people harnesses the strength of diversity, bringing together a variety of perspectives, experiences, and expertise to combat racism effectively. Such collaboration promotes a more comprehensive understanding of racial issues and facilitates the development of intersectional solutions that address the unique challenges faced by different communities.

Through collaboration, BIPOC and White people can amplify each other's voices, working toward breaking down barriers and dismantling systems of racial oppression. This alliance enables White individuals to leverage their privilege and become anti-racist advocates and allies who actively challenge and confront racism within their communities.

Cross-cultural Understanding and Empathy

Collaboration on anti-racism necessitates an active commitment to understanding and dismantling stereotypes and prejudices held by both BIPOC and White people. By engaging in open dialogues, listening to each other's stories, sharing experiences of discrimination, and acknowledging one's own biases, individuals can work toward fostering empathy and bridging gaps in understanding. Collaboration requires White people to be willing to create spaces where BIPOC voices are centered and respected. By actively uplifting and amplifying the experiences, perspectives, and achievements of BIPOC individuals, White allies can transform dialogue into action, creating a more inclusive and equitable society. Collaboration allows for cultural exchange, which is an essential component of anti-racism work. BIPOC and White people can engage in mutual learning, understanding, and appreciation of each other's cultures, dismantling stereotypes and fostering a sense of shared humanity.

Moreover, anti-racism promotes empathy by encouraging individuals to understand marginalized groups' experiences, emotions, and struggles. It challenges bias, stereotypes, and prejudice, allowing people to develop a genuine connection with diverse communities. Through empathy, individuals become more open-minded and willing to challenge their own biases, thus creating a culture of understanding and respect. By fostering empathy, anti-racism helps bridge racial divides and builds strong social cohesion, fostering a sense of belonging for all members of society.

Shared Goals and Systemic Change

Collaboration on anti-racism aims to tackle deeply embedded structural racism that permeates society. By identifying common goals, such as equal access to education, economic opportunities, and justice, BIPOC and White people can work together to eradicate systemic racism and achieve racial equity. Collaboration between BIPOC and White people is pivotal in lobbying for legislative reforms and policy changes that address racially biased practices and policies. By sharing resources, advocating for policy reforms, and supporting anti-racist political candidates, this collaboration can drive sustainable changes on a systemic level.

Collaboration enables the development of educational initiatives to address racial biases and create awareness among individuals from all racial backgrounds. By jointly organizing workshops, conferences, and community programs, both White and BIPOC individuals can contribute to educating society about the impact of racism and promoting a more inclusive, compassionate, and anti-racist future.

Anti-racism plays a crucial role in driving social progress by dismantling oppressive structures and challenging societal norms that perpetuate racist behaviors. It sheds light on the injustices marginalized groups face, forcing societies to confront their biases and work toward rectifying them. Anti-racism initiatives encourage dialogue, education, and awareness, allowing individuals to challenge institutionalized racism and advocate for lasting change. By acknowledging and addressing systemic racism, societies can pave the way for a more just, inclusive, and prosperous future.

Finally, collaboration on anti-racism between BIPOC and White people is essential to bring about meaningful change that dismantles systemic racism.

By fostering understanding, empathy, and shared goals, this collaboration has the potential to unite individuals from diverse backgrounds, amplify voices, challenge prejudices, and drive legislative and systemic reforms. By pursuing collective action, we can strive toward a world that acknowledges the pain and injustices caused by racism and actively works toward a more equitable and just society for all.

Social Justice in Racial Inclusion

Social justice in the context of racial inclusion suggests that social justice and racial inclusion interact together to create a society with equity and justice.

Social justice is a fundamental principle that encompasses fair and impartial treatment for all members of society. Achieving a just society requires addressing the disparities among different racial groups. Racial inclusion is crucial to social justice, ensuring that individuals from diverse racial backgrounds have equitable access to resources, opportunities, and social benefits. The various dimensions of racial inclusion can be achieved through social justice for marginalized racial groups.

The increase in social justice is another benefit of racial inclusion. The multifaceted aspects of increasing social justice benefit society in numerous ways. By examining the benefits of enhanced social justice, we can better understand its positive impacts on various aspects of society, including education, employment, healthcare, and overall well-being. It is crucial to acknowledge that achieving social justice is a continuous work in progress and requires concerted efforts at both individual and systemic levels. However, the rewards of increased social justice are immense and can contribute to a fairer and more harmonious society.

Increased social justice may come from education, promoting students' equity awareness. Enhancing social justice benefits in education is paramount for providing equal educational opportunities to all individuals. Education is a powerful tool for empowering individuals, breaking the cycle of poverty, and offering avenues for upward social mobility. By advocating for increased social justice in education, marginalized groups can receive the necessary resources, quality teaching, and supportive environments to thrive academically. This will contribute to more equitable outcomes and reduce educational disparities.

Increased social justice helps reduce health disparities. Access to quality healthcare is a fundamental human right, yet it is not distributed in many societies. By increasing social justice benefits in healthcare, marginalized groups can have equal access to essential medical services, preventive care, and health education. This will help address health disparities and improve overall population health outcomes. Furthermore, increasing social justice benefits in healthcare can also provide mental health support to vulnerable populations. Mental health is integral to overall well-being and deserves equal attention and resources. By ensuring access to mental health services, marginalized individuals can receive the support they need, leading to improved overall mental and emotional well-being.

When social justice increases, the benefits in various domains ultimately contribute to individuals' overall well-being and happiness, and such happiness further promotes racial inclusion. When societies are characterized by fairness, inclusivity, and equal opportunities, a collective sense of social cohesion enhances overall well-being. People feel valued, acknowledged, and respected, fostering a sense of belonging and fulfillment.

In sum, social justice creates numerous benefits, from individuals to the system. Social justice is also a beneficial and positive example of racial inclusion. Increasing social justice benefits across different domains of society is a crucial step toward building a fairer and more just world. Increased social justice benefits and promotes education, employment, healthcare, and overall well-being. Achieving social justice remains an ongoing endeavor, requiring continuous efforts in policymaking, educational reforms, inclusive practices, and societal awareness. However, the rewards of enhanced social justice are invaluable, as they create a more equitable and harmonious society where every individual can reach their full potential.

Chapter 5

Challenges in the Transformation from Racial Discrimination to Racial Inclusion

The process of transformation encounters various challenges. The transformation from racial discrimination to racial inclusion is a change process for the better. In our society, transformation from racial discrimination to racial inclusion often refers to improving systems, institutions, and practices to achieve progress and desired outcomes. However, this process can be incredibly challenging, especially when addressing complex issues that persist within our communities.

PROCESS OF TRANSFORMATION

One of the primary challenges in transformation is the complexity of the issues at hand. Often, the transformations required to address these issues involve multiple stakeholders, intricate systems, and deep-rooted problems that have existed for years or even decades. For example, transforming education systems to cater to diverse student needs, enhance inclusivity, and provide equitable opportunities is complex. Such transformations require altering curriculum, teacher training, and administrative processes, among other aspects.

Furthermore, these challenges can be amplified when addressing social issues such as inequality, poverty, or environmental sustainability. These problems are interconnected and multifaceted, requiring a holistic approach to transformation. It becomes imperative to consider the intersectionality of various factors contributing to these issues and to develop comprehensive strategies for transformation.

Stage 1: Awareness and Self-reflection

The process of transformation begins with the crucial step of self-awareness. This involves recognizing the need for change and reflecting on one's aspirations, values, strengths, and weaknesses. Through introspection and self-evaluation, individuals understand their current situation and identify areas that require improvement. This stage lays the foundation for the subsequent steps, as it engenders a genuine desire for personal growth.

Racial inclusion has emerged as a critical topic of discussion within various communities and academic circles. As society becomes more diverse and interconnected, promoting and advocating for racial inclusion is essential to building a harmonious and inclusive society. However, achieving racial inclusion is not a simple task; it requires individuals to undergo a process of self-reflection and develop an awareness of their biases and privileges. A few challenges are still faced during this process, highlighting the importance of awareness and self-reflection for racial inclusion at the education level.

To understand the challenges in awareness and self-reflection for racial inclusion, it is crucial to acknowledge the historical context of racism and discrimination. Deep-rooted biases and prejudices originating from historical events, such as colonization and racial segregation, continue to influence individuals' perspectives. This historical baggage presents a significant hurdle in understanding and accepting racial diversity.

One of the primary challenges in fostering racial inclusion lies in addressing implicit biases and unconscious prejudices. Implicit biases are deeply ingrained associations people make between social groups and certain traits, which can influence their judgments and behaviors, often without conscious awareness. Overcoming these biases requires individuals to engage in self-reflection and acknowledge their existence.

Another challenge is limited awareness. Many individuals, particularly those who belong to racially privileged groups, may lack awareness of the challenges faced by racial minorities. This limited awareness can hinder efforts toward racial inclusion, as it prevents individuals from developing empathy and understanding. Educators play a crucial role in exposing students to diverse perspectives and experiences, enabling them to develop a broader awareness of racial issues.

Addressing racial inclusion evokes emotional resistance among White people who are uncomfortable acknowledging their privileges or confronting the negative aspects of their racial identities. This resistance can manifest as defensiveness or denial, hindering progress toward self-reflection and meaningful dialogue. Overcoming emotional resistance calls for a safe and inclusive environment where individuals can openly express their emotions and concerns.

The education system is pivotal in fostering awareness and self-reflection for racial inclusion. However, it also faces inherent challenges that need to be addressed. Curriculum biases, a lack of diverse representation in teaching materials, and the absence of comprehensive anti-racism education hinder the development of awareness among people. Reforming the education system to include comprehensive racial studies and diverse representation is vital for promoting self-reflection and fostering racial inclusion.

Another significant challenge is the need for meaningful dialogue and collaboration between racial groups. Open and constructive conversations are crucial for addressing biases, dispelling misconceptions, and fostering understanding. However, the fear of saying the wrong thing or being labeled prejudiced often stifles dialogue. Encouraging safe spaces for conversation, active listening, and empathetic engagement can help overcome this challenge.

Resistance to change is another form of lack of awareness and self-reflection. Lack of awareness is a significant obstacle in transforming systems and practices. Humans are creatures of habit, and there is often a natural aversion to moving away from familiar routines and structures. This resistance can arise from a fear of the unknown, concerns about the potential consequences of change, or a lack of awareness about the benefits of transformation.

In many cases, those who benefit from the current state of affairs may oppose transformation because they fear losing their privileges or power. This resistance may manifest in various forms, such as bureaucratic barriers, lack of stakeholder cooperation, or even political opposition. Overcoming this resistance requires effective leadership, communication, and an emphasis on the benefits and positive outcomes that can result from the transformation process.

As we discussed in chapter 1, it is not uncommon to encounter emotional resistance or defensiveness when discussing race-related issues and racial inclusion. Resistance to change in attitudes and behaviors is a common challenge in promoting racial inclusion. Many individuals prefer the status quo and find comfort in maintaining power dynamics that favor their racial group. Overcoming this resistance requires persistent efforts to challenge and dismantle systemic racism, both on an individual and institutional level.

Stage 2: Setting Clear Goals

Once individuals have gained clarity about themselves, they can set clear and attainable goals. Goals act as a roadmap for transformation, providing direction and focus. Setting goals allows individuals to envision their desired future state and establish a sense of purpose. It is essential for goals to be specific, measurable, achievable, relevant, and time-bound (SMART) to ensure effective transformation.

Despite it being clear that racial inclusion is a fundamental aspect of any society that strives to achieve equality and justice for all its members, setting clear goals for racial inclusion poses numerous challenges, particularly in addressing the deep-rooted systemic issues that perpetuate racial discrimination and inequality. The challenges in setting clear goals in transforming to racial inclusion also indicate a lack of collaboration and consensus in the goals and targets between BIPOC and White people.

One of the significant challenges in setting clear goals for racial inclusion is the historical context of racial discrimination and inequality. In history, BIPOC individuals and communities have initiated the change toward racial inclusion due to the racial oppression they suffer. Many societies have a long history of racial oppression, where certain racial groups have been systematically marginalized and denied equal opportunities, rights, and representation. Overcoming the effects of this historical context requires a comprehensive understanding of the dynamics that perpetuate racial inequality. However, determining clear goals that work effectively for both BIPOC and White people to address these issues can be difficult due to the complexity of historical legacies and the necessity of understanding the multifaceted factors that contribute to racial discrimination.

Another challenge in setting clear goals for racial inclusion is the limited resources available to address these issues. Achieving meaningful racial inclusion requires substantial education, social programs, and investment in support systems. However, limited financial resources often hinder the implementation of comprehensive strategies. Additionally, the scarcity of resources can lead to a prioritization dilemma, with different stakeholders advocating for different approaches or areas of focus. As a result, setting clear goals that effectively allocate these limited resources becomes a complex task.

Transforming systems and institutions often requires significant resources, including financial, human, and technological resources. Adequate funding is crucial to implementing changes effectively, whether they involve infrastructure modifications, training programs, or research initiatives. Moreover, lacking skilled personnel or expertise in specific areas can hinder the transformation process.

Resource constraints can severely limit the scope and pace of transformation, especially in developing countries or disadvantaged communities. Addressing this challenge calls for innovative solutions, such as public-private partnerships, international collaborations, and leveraging technology to bridge resource gaps. Additionally, capacity-building efforts and investing in education and skills development can empower individuals and communities to drive transformation processes with limited resources.

One of the most significant challenges in setting clear goals for racial inclusion is societal resistance. Despite progress in civil rights movements and anti-discrimination legislation, there is still widespread resistance to change among individuals and institutions. This resistance can manifest in various ways, such as discriminatory practices, biased attitudes, and systemic barriers. Overcoming societal resistance requires a comprehensive and systematic approach that addresses implicit biases, promotes diversity and inclusion in institutions, and promotes intercultural understanding. However, setting clear goals that effectively combat these profoundly ingrained attitudes and behaviors can be challenging, as they require significant changes in societal structures and individual mindsets.

The complex nature of racial dynamics presents another challenge in setting clear goals for racial inclusion. Racial inequalities are not limited to single events or isolated incidents but are deeply embedded in all aspects of society, including education, employment, housing, and the criminal justice system. This complexity necessitates a thorough understanding of the interactions between factors contributing to racial inequality. However, setting clear goals in addressing these complex dynamics can be challenging, as it requires developing comprehensive strategies that consider the intersections of race with other social factors such as gender, class, and immigration status.

Finally, setting clear goals for racial inclusion is crucial for promoting equality and justice for all members of society. However, numerous challenges hinder the establishment of practical goals in addressing racial discrimination. Overcoming historical legacies, limited resources, societal resistance, and the complex nature of racial dynamics requires a comprehensive and multifaceted approach. By recognizing and understanding these challenges, societies can develop more precise goals and strategies to promote racial inclusion and equality. It is essential to acknowledge that setting clear goals alone is not sufficient; a continuous commitment to addressing racial discrimination is necessary to ensure progress and improve the lives of all individuals impacted by racial inequality.

Stage 3: Acquiring Knowledge and Skills

Transformation often necessitates the acquisition of new knowledge and skills. Individuals seeking personal growth invest time and effort in acquiring education, training, or specialized knowledge relevant to their goals. This step may involve pursuing formal education, attending workshops, engaging in mentoring relationships, or self-directed learning. Acquiring knowledge and skills equips individuals with the necessary tools to overcome challenges and achieve their goals. Acquiring knowledge and skills in racial inclusion is crucial in promoting diversity, understanding different perspectives, and combating racism. However, there are several challenges that educators and learners face in acquiring this knowledge and developing skills related to racial inclusion. One of the primary challenges is acquiring knowledge and skills about transforming to racial inclusion. Society is often built on stereotypes and prejudices, which can hinder learning. Sometimes, individuals may not even realize the gravity or impact of their biases on others. This lack of knowledge makes creating an inclusive environment and engaging in meaningful dialogue difficult.

Another challenge lies in educators' competence and training in addressing issues of racial inclusion. Often, educators may not possess the necessary knowledge or skills to navigate discussions about race and ethnicity effectively. They may struggle with discussing sensitive topics, unknowingly perpetuate biases, or lack the tools to create inclusive learning spaces. This inadequacy in educator training can hinder the transmission of knowledge and skills related to racial inclusion.

The curriculum and educational resources used in educational institutions significantly shape people's understanding of racial inclusion. However, in some cases, the curriculum may lack diverse perspectives or even perpetuate stereotypes. This can hinder the acquisition of knowledge and skills in racial inclusion. Additionally, the lack of educational resources that address racial inclusion or offer diverse perspectives limits students' exposure to these essential topics.

Acquiring knowledge and skills in racial inclusion can face resistance and pushback from various segments of society. Some individuals may view discussions about racism and inclusion as unnecessary or even perceive them as threatening their own beliefs and privileges. This resistance can create a hostile learning environment, making it challenging for people to engage in open dialogue and acquire the necessary knowledge and skills related to racial inclusion.

The above challenges are actually opportunities for BPIC and White people to work together to create solutions. While the challenges in acquiring knowledge and skills in racial inclusion are significant, there are potential solutions that can help overcome them. First, raising awareness and understanding is essential. Educators and learners need to engage in open and honest conversations about race, stereotypes, and biases. This can be achieved through diversity training programs and workshops, as well as by incorporating literature and resources that reflect diverse perspectives into the curriculum.

Second, enhancing educator competence and training is crucial. Professional development programs should be designed to equip educators with the necessary tools and skills to address racial inclusion effectively. This training can include understanding cultural differences, promoting empathy, and creating inclusive classroom environments.

Third, revising the curriculum and educational resources is essential. Educational institutions should strive to provide a curriculum that includes diverse perspectives, histories, and cultures. This can be done by reviewing and revising existing curriculum materials or incorporating new resources that promote understanding and acceptance. By doing so, learners will have the opportunity to acquire knowledge and skills related to racial inclusion.

Lastly, addressing resistance and pushback requires creating safe spaces for dialogue. Open and respectful discussions must be fostered, allowing individuals to express their concerns, fears, and perspectives. Educators and institutions should emphasize the importance of inclusion and provide the necessary support for those who may feel threatened or uncomfortable with these discussions.

Stage 4: Taking Action

Taking action is a critical step in the transformation process, as it involves implementing plans and making tangible progress toward one's goals. Overcoming obstacles and setbacks along the way requires courage, perseverance, and resilience. By consistently taking action, individuals begin to witness small successes, which further fuel their motivation to continue with the transformative journey.

Achieving racial inclusion necessitates a proactive approach that addresses the challenges and barriers hindering progress. A few challenges are faced in addressing racial inclusion and discussing the complexities and strategies required to promote equality and harmony among diverse racial groups.

One of the most prominent challenges to racial inclusion lies within the structural and systemic racism deeply ingrained in societies. Institutional frameworks, policies, and practices have often led to the perpetuation of racial disparities and unequal opportunities. Remedying these deeply rooted biases requires comprehensive reforms in education, employment, housing, and criminal justice systems.

Unconscious biases and stereotypes continue to hinder racial inclusion efforts. These biases can manifest in various ways, such as discriminatory hiring practices or negative portrayals of racial groups in the media. Addressing implicit bias necessitates raising awareness, implementing diversity training programs, and actively challenging stereotypes to promote inclusivity effectively.

The need for more diverse representation in positions of power and decision-making poses another challenge to achieving racial inclusion. When the voices and experiences of marginalized racial groups are not adequately represented, policies and initiatives aimed at equality may not adequately address the specific needs and challenges these groups face. Promoting representation at all levels of society is crucial to dismantling systemic barriers and fostering racial inclusion.

Despite significant progress, overt acts of prejudice and discrimination persist in society, hindering genuine efforts toward racial inclusion. Hate crimes, racial slurs, and racially motivated violence are just some examples of the entrenched prejudices that impede racial progress. Combating racism requires a multifaceted approach involving education, law enforcement, and community engagement to challenge such behaviors and create a culture of acceptance and respect.

Stage 5: Accountability and Evaluation

Accountability plays a vital role in ensuring the sustainability of the transformative process. Individuals benefit from developing accountability systems by sharing their goals with trusted individuals or joining support groups. These mechanisms create a sense of responsibility and facilitate ongoing motivation and progress. Additionally, regular evaluation allows individuals to assess their progress, identify areas for improvement, and make necessary adjustments to achieve their desired outcomes.

In recent years, there has been a growing recognition of the need to ensure equal opportunities and representation for all racial and ethnic groups. Governments, organizations, and educational institutions have initiated policies and programs to promote racial inclusion. However, the effectiveness of these initiatives is often challenged by a lack of accountability and evaluation measures.

One of the key challenges in accountability lies in defining clear and measurable goals for racial inclusion. While the goal of achieving racial equity is widely acknowledged, the specific objectives and outcomes of inclusion initiatives often need to be more specific and clear. This lack of clarity makes it difficult to hold individuals, organizations, or governments accountable for their actions and progress toward racial inclusion. Additionally, accountability mechanisms may need to be more well-defined and implemented, allowing for a lack of transparency and responsibility.

Another challenge is the resistance or hesitancy to accept accountability for racial inclusion. Some individuals or organizations may view racial inclusion as a threat to their power or privilege, leading to a reluctance to actively participate in measures promoting inclusivity. This can hinder progress and perpetuate systems of inequality.

Practical evaluation is crucial for determining the impact and success of racial inclusion initiatives. However, there are several challenges in conducting comprehensive evaluations. First, evaluating racial inclusion is complex due to various socioeconomic, cultural, and historical factors. Discrimination and inequality are deeply rooted in societies, making it difficult to measure the accurate outcomes of inclusion efforts. Moreover, individual experiences of racial exclusion or discrimination are subjective and contextual, making it challenging to develop standardized evaluation tools.

Another challenge is the need for more data and evidence to inform the evaluation process. Racial and ethnic data collection can be limited or inadequate, preventing a comprehensive understanding of the extent of racial inclusion and its impact. Additionally, cultural and language barriers may impede accurate data collection, further complicating the evaluation processes.

Furthermore, evaluating inclusivity initiatives requires a long-term perspective. Sustainable change takes time, making it difficult to measure short-term outcomes. Many initiatives addressing racial inclusion require continuous efforts and resources, making it challenging to demonstrate immediate progress.

Several strategies can be implemented to overcome the challenges of accountability and evaluation in racial inclusion. First, clear and measurable goals need to be established, outlining specific objectives and outcomes. These goals should be communicated widely to ensure a shared understanding and commitment to racial inclusion.

Transparency and effective communication are also essential for accountability. Governments, organizations, and individuals involved in racial inclusion initiatives should provide regular updates and reports on their progress. Creating open dialogue and feedback platforms can encourage stakeholders to take responsibility and actively engage in inclusion efforts.

Reliable data on racial demographics and experiences is crucial for addressing evaluation challenges. Governments and organizations should invest in improving data collection methods, ensuring the inclusion of diverse racial and ethnic groups. Collaborations with academic institutions and researchers can facilitate the development of standardized evaluation tools that consider racial inclusion's interdisciplinary and contextual nature.

Evaluation processes should also take into account long-term impact and effectiveness. Emphasizing qualitative data collection, such as individual stories and experiences, can provide a deeper understanding of the progress and challenges faced in achieving racial inclusion.

Stage 6: Integration and Consolidation

As individuals move toward the final stages of transformation, they integrate their newfound knowledge, skills, and experiences into their daily lives. This stage involves consciously incorporating the changes and lessons learned into various aspects of life—personal, professional, and social. The integration phase assists in anchoring transformation as a permanent part of one's identity, ensuring long-term growth and development.

Another critical challenge is ensuring that the transformations pursued are sustainable and scalable. Often, initiatives fail to produce lasting change due to a lack of foresight regarding their long-term impact. For instance, a successful pilot project in one school may struggle to replicate the same results across an entire district or country. Sustainability in transformation efforts requires careful planning, monitoring, evaluation, and building capacity at all levels.

Moreover, considering the impacts of transformations on future generations is crucial. More is needed to ensure short-term benefits; the focus should also be on creating a system that can adapt and evolve to meet society's changing needs and demands. This requires integrating social, economic, and environmental sustainability into the transformation agenda.

To reach racial inclusion, integrating and consolidating different racial groups is a complex but necessary goal. Achieving racial inclusion requires deliberate efforts to create equitable opportunities and address systemic barriers perpetuating inequalities. However, numerous challenges hinder the progress toward racial inclusion, such as deep-rooted prejudices, institutional discrimination, lack of policy implementation, and socioeconomic disparities.

Integration and consolidation in racial inclusion are fundamental to building a just and inclusive society. As the world becomes more multicultural, it is essential to address discrimination and exclusion faced by marginalized racial groups. Racism and racial inequalities have been deeply embedded in societies worldwide for centuries, resulting in an ongoing struggle for racial inclusion. There are challenges faced in integrating and consolidating racial inclusion, highlighting their impact, and suggesting potential solutions.

One of the primary challenges to racial inclusion is profoundly ingrained prejudice and stereotyping. People often hold biases and stereotypes about racial minorities, perpetuating a narrative that depicts them as inferior or threatening. These biases lead to discrimination, exclusion, and marginalization, hindering integration efforts. Overcoming these biases requires conscious efforts to challenge and unlearn them through education, dialogue, and exposure to diverse perspectives.

Institutional discrimination entails the systemic biases and barriers that racially marginalized communities encounter in various domains of life, such as education, employment, housing, and criminal justice. These institutions perpetuate racial inequalities, making it challenging for individuals from minority backgrounds to access opportunities equally. Addressing institutional discrimination demands comprehensive reforms and policies that challenge discriminatory practices and prioritize equity.

Although many countries have implemented anti-discrimination laws and policies to promote racial inclusion, the lack of proper implementation poses a significant challenge. Governments may pass legislation and establish institutions, but with effective execution, marginalized communities can avoid exclusion and discrimination. Strengthening the enforcement of existing policies and creating mechanisms for monitoring their implementation is crucial for achieving racial inclusion.

Racial inequalities are often intertwined with socioeconomic disparities. Minorities typically face disproportionately high poverty rates and limited access to education, healthcare, and stable employment. These disparities hinder integration as marginalized communities struggle to break free from systemic cycles of poverty and exclusion. Addressing socioeconomic disparities requires targeted interventions such as affirmative action, equal opportunities for employment and education, and inclusive economic policies.

STAGES OF CHANGE FOR THE TRANSFORMATION FROM RACIAL DISCRIMINATION TO RACIAL INCLUSION

The concept of change is inherent to individuals' growth and development. Whether it is a personal transformation or an organizational shift, change is necessary for progress and improvement. The stages of change model in education have gained significant attention as a framework for understanding behavior modification and how it can impact student learning outcomes.

The stages of change model, also known as the transtheoretical model, was first proposed by Prochaska and DiClemente in the late 1970s to describe and explain the process of intentional behavior change. Initially formulated to study the process of smoking cessation, this model was later applied to various health-related behaviors such as substance abuse, diet, exercise, and mental health. Over time, researchers and theorists recognized its relevance in educational settings, which led to the development of the stages of change model in education.

The stages of change model posits that individuals undergo a series of stages when modifying their behavior. These stages include pre-contemplation, contemplation, preparation, action, maintenance, and termination. The pre-contemplation stage represents a lack of awareness or recognition of the need for change, while contemplation involves weighing the pros and cons of the behavior change. Preparation signifies the intention to act and develop a plan, followed by the action stage, where the individual engages in the desired behavior modification. Maintenance involves sustaining the behavior change over time, and the termination stage reflects a complete integration of the change into one's life.

Pre-contemplation Stage

In the pre-contemplation stage, people may not recognize the need for educational change or feel complacent with their current situation. Educators can engage students at this stage by raising awareness of potential benefits, highlighting the gap between their current state and their desired goals, and providing relevant information as motivation for contemplation. Racial inclusion refers to creating an inclusive society that embraces diversity, promotes equal opportunities, and eliminates discriminatory practices. In the pre-contemplation stage of racial inclusion, the focus is on understanding the various barriers that hinder progress and exploring strategies for initiating change within the educational research thesis. In the context of racial inclusion, the pre-contemplation stage involves individuals who do not perceive or understand the importance of racial inclusion and its impact on society.

Barriers to Racial Inclusion

Several barriers contribute to the pre-contemplation stage in racial inclusion. First, historical and social factors such as colonialism, slavery, and segregation have perpetuated systemic racism, leading to the normalization of discriminatory practices within various institutions. This normalization creates a mindset that inhibits individuals from recognizing the need for change and embracing racial inclusion. Second, ignorance and lack of awareness play a significant role in maintaining the pre-contemplation stage. Many individuals may not have exposure to diverse populations, limiting their understanding of the challenges faced by racial minorities. Ignorance often stems from a lack of education and knowledge surrounding racism and its detrimental consequences on society, hindering individuals from acknowledging the need for change.

Moreover, fear and resistance of White people to change act as psychological barriers to racial inclusion. People might fear losing their privilege or perceive racial inclusion as a threat to their existing beliefs and ways of life. This fear and resistance to change reinforce the pre-contemplation stage, thereby impeding progress toward a more inclusive society.

Solutions for Initiating Change

To address the pre-contemplation stage in racial inclusion, it is crucial to develop strategies that foster awareness, educate individuals, and challenge existing biases. Education plays a pivotal role as a catalyst for change. An educational research thesis can actively examine and challenge the prevailing racial narratives, generating empirical evidence supporting the need for racial inclusion.

First, educational institutions should prioritize incorporating diverse perspectives and experiences into curriculum design, ensuring that people are exposed to different cultures and histories. This approach nurtures a positive learning environment that fosters empathy, respect, and understanding among people, subsequently breaking down the pre-contemplation stage.

Second, outreach programs, community engagement, and dialogue platforms should be established to create spaces for open conversations about race and racial inclusion. These initiatives can serve as catalysts for promoting awareness and overcoming resistance to change. Public figures, policymakers, and leaders should partake in these discussions to demonstrate their commitment to the cause and offer guidance on bringing about meaningful change.

Third, media and popular culture platforms can be harnessed to challenge stereotypes and promote positive portrayals of diverse racial groups. Representational diversity in films, TV shows, and literature can contribute to erasing preconceived notions and the ultimate acceptance of racial inclusion.

Contemplation Stage

During the contemplation stage, people become aware of the necessity for change but may struggle to commit to it. Educators play a crucial role at this stage by encouraging exploration, supporting decision-making, and offering resources that aid people in clarifying their goals.

The contemplation stage in racial inclusion is when an individual or an institution begins to seriously consider and reflect upon the need for incorporating racial diversity and equality. This stage is crucial as it lays the foundation for meaningful changes in society and institutions. However, numerous challenges arise during this contemplation stage, hindering progress toward racial inclusion.

Obstacles to Racial Inclusion

One of the primary obstacles in the contemplation stage is the need for more awareness and understanding of the necessity for racial inclusion. Many individuals and organizations may need to recognize the disparities or biases in their communities or systems. Overcoming this challenge involves creating platforms for open dialogue and promoting education on racial history, privilege, and social justice. Awareness campaigns, diversity training programs, and inclusivity workshops can play a vital role in fostering a deeper understanding of the importance of racial inclusion.

Resistance to change is another significant obstacle encountered during the contemplation stage. Individuals and institutions that have benefited from the existing racial hierarchy may be hesitant to challenge their privilege. This resistance stems from fear, ignorance, or a desire to maintain the status quo. Encouraging a mindset of inclusivity requires addressing this resistance through active engagement, empathy, and the promotion of shared values that prioritize fairness and equity. Promoting the advantages of diversity and providing evidence of its positive impact can help alleviate this resistance.

The sociopolitical climate can profoundly influence the contemplation stage of racial inclusion. Racial tension, discrimination, or social unrest can act as catalysts or barriers to initiating change. For instance, racial justice movements such as Black Lives Matter have sparked widespread contemplation and conversations on racial inclusion. However, a divisive political climate may impede progress, as it may further polarize discussions and hinder constructive dialogue on racial equality. Overcoming this challenge necessitates building bridges across ideological divides, fostering empathy, and emphasizing the shared goal of societal progress.

Leadership commitment is vital during the contemplation stage as it sets the tone and agenda for progressing toward racial inclusion. However, a lack of commitment from leaders and decision-makers can undermine efforts for change. This challenge can be addressed through accountability mechanisms that hold leaders responsible for fostering racial inclusion within their organizations or institutions. Additionally, creating platforms for diverse voices to influence decision-making processes is crucial to ensure the incorporation of varied perspectives and ideas.

Solution

Implementing racial inclusion initiatives often requires resources such as funding, staff, and time commitment. Limited resources can pose challenges during the contemplation stage, as resources may not be prioritized for diversity and inclusion efforts. Overcoming this hurdle necessitates showcasing the long-term benefits of racial inclusion, developing strategic plans that utilize existing resources efficiently, and seeking external support through partnerships or grants. Prioritizing budgetary allocations that reflect the commitment to racial inclusion helps create sustainable change.

A primary solution is to address systemic barriers. Institutions must introspectively evaluate existing policies, practices, and attitudes that perpetuate racial inequality. This may involve conducting comprehensive equity audits and revising admission processes, curriculum, and disciplinary policies. By rectifying unjust practices, educational institutions can create an inclusive environment that values diversity and eliminates discriminatory barriers.

Cultural competence is essential for promoting racial inclusion. Educational institutions should prioritize promoting cultural diversity and multicultural understanding among students and staff members. One strategy to achieve this is to implement comprehensive diversity training programs that provide individuals with the knowledge, skills, and attitudes necessary for fostering an inclusive environment. These programs should address implicit biases, cultural stereotyping, and microaggressions. Furthermore, institutions can establish multicultural clubs and organizations, organize cultural events, and collaborate with communities to create cross-cultural learning and engagement opportunities.

Representation plays a pivotal role in racial inclusion efforts. Increasing the representation of marginalized communities among teachers, administrators, and staff members is crucial for fostering an inclusive environment. Through targeted recruitment efforts and mentorship programs, institutions can encourage individuals from diverse racial backgrounds to pursue careers in education. Moreover, amplifying the voices and perspectives of marginalized communities through curriculum development, guest speakers, and inclusive learning materials can help dismantle existing structures of power and promote understanding and empathy.

Community engagement is another critical solution in the contemplation stage of racial inclusion efforts. Educational institutions should actively seek partnerships with local organizations and community leaders to develop strategies addressing racial education disparities. Collaborative projects, such as mentoring programs, college access initiatives, and community-based learning opportunities, can bridge the gap between schools and communities. By involving parents, families, and community members in decision-making, institutions can create a shared vision for racial inclusion and collectively work toward its realization.

Preparation Stage

The preparation stage is marked by individuals making active plans to initiate change. People may need assistance identifying appropriate courses, programs, or educational strategies to match their desired goals. Educators can provide guidance, mentorship, and necessary resources to support people in effectively preparing for the next stage. Racial inclusion is critical to modern society, ensuring equal opportunities and fair representation for individuals of all races and ethnicities. Achieving racial inclusion requires a well-planned and executed preparation stage that addresses the challenges inherent in this process.

Challenges

One of the fundamental challenges in the preparation stage of racial inclusion is the need for more awareness and understanding among individuals and institutions. In many cases, people are unaware of the historical and sociopolitical contexts that have shaped racial inequalities, leading to a dismissive attitude or an oversimplified understanding of the issues at hand. Consequently, efforts to prepare for racial inclusion often face resistance or a shallow commitment to change.

Resistance and opposition to racial inclusion initiatives pose significant challenges during the preparation stage. Individuals and institutions with vested interests in maintaining the status quo may resist change due to fear, bias, or a perceived loss of power or privilege. Such resistance hampers the preparation process by impeding dialogue, collaboration, and the development of inclusive policies and practices.

Institutional barriers are a significant challenge in the preparation stage of racial inclusion. Institutions, including educational establishments, often have deeply entrenched structures, policies, and procedures that perpetuate racial disparities. Overcoming these barriers requires a comprehensive assessment of existing practices, policies, and curricula to identify and rectify systemic biases and discriminatory practices that hinder inclusion efforts.

More resources, both financial and human, pose another challenge in the preparation stage of racial inclusion. Addressing inequalities, developing anti-racist curricula, and implementing diversity training programs require substantial investments of time, money, and expertise. Limited resources can impede progress and create barriers, as institutions may need help to allocate the necessary funds and personnel to support these initiatives.

An essential aspect of the preparation stage for racial inclusion is the development of cultural competence. However, many education systems must adequately prepare teachers and administrators to effectively engage with diverse student populations. Cultural competence training is necessary to equip education professionals with the skills, knowledge, and sensitivity to address racial disparities and foster an inclusive learning environment.

Curriculum reform is essential to preparing for racial inclusion, yet it often faces resistance from various stakeholders. Traditional curricula tend to perpetuate dominant narratives, often marginalizing the contributions and experiences of racial minorities. Overcoming resistance to curriculum change requires extensive dialogue, collaboration, and a commitment to challenging traditional perspectives to ensure a comprehensive and representative education for all people.

Solutions

Overcoming these challenges requires a comprehensive and strategic approach that prioritizes education, awareness, and the development of inclusive policies and practices. Addressing the lack of awareness and understanding, resistance and opposition, institutional barriers, limited resources, the need for cultural competence training, and resistance to curriculum change are crucial. By doing so, society can progress toward racial inclusion, fostering a more equitable and inclusive future for all.

Action Stage

In the action stage, individuals actively engage in implementing their educational plans. Educators can provide ongoing feedback, monitor progress, and address challenges or obstacles encountered along the way. This stage demands institutional support and resources to ensure that people stay motivated and achieve their goals.

The pursuit of racial inclusion within societies has become a paramount issue across the globe. Education serves as a vital platform for creating an inclusive environment, promoting social equality, and fostering an understanding of different cultures. However, the action stage of racial inclusion presents many challenges that hinder the implementation of effective policies and initiatives. A detailed analysis of the challenges encountered during the action stage of racial inclusion, specifically within the realm of transformation, will help us prepare to create solutions to overcome these challenges.

Challenges

One of the primary challenges in the action stage of racial inclusion is the deep-seated cultural bias and stereotypes that exist in educational systems. Such bias affects student-teacher relationships and shapes curriculum content and teaching approaches. Stereotypes perpetuated through textbooks, teaching materials, and disciplinary methods reinforce racial inequalities and hinder progress toward racial inclusion. Overcoming these deeply ingrained biases requires a collective effort from policymakers, educators, and administrators alike.

A significant challenge faced in the racial inclusion action stage is insufficient representation and diversity within the curriculum. The traditional curriculum often fails to incorporate the contributions and perspectives of racial minorities, thus perpetuating stereotypes and marginalization. By incorporating diverse voices and experiences, people can develop a broader understanding and appreciation of different cultures. However, implementing an inclusive curriculum requires addressing the systemic biases and resistance to change within educational institutions.

Educators are crucial in shaping people's perceptions and attitudes toward racial inclusion. However, many teachers are ill-equipped to address the complexities of racial diversity in the classroom due to insufficient training and professional development opportunities. This lack of preparation hampers their ability to create a supportive and inclusive learning environment. Comprehensive training programs addressing cultural competency and anti-bias education are essential to foster racial inclusion within educational settings.

Institutional racism and discrimination pose significant challenges in the action stage of racial inclusion. These systemic barriers hinder marginalized people's access to quality education, perpetuating the racial achievement gap. Discrimination within disciplinary practices and school policies further marginalizes minority people, leading to disproportionate rates of exclusion and punishment. Addressing institutional racism requires a comprehensive approach involving policy reforms, inclusive leadership, and safe spaces within educational institutions.

The action stage of racial inclusion is hindered by the need for more resources and funding directed toward initiatives that promote diversity and inclusion in education. Educational institutions serving racially diverse populations often lack resources, resulting in limited access to quality educational materials, technology, and specialized programs. Adequate funding is critical to implement targeted interventions, hire diverse staff, and provide necessary resources to enhance teaching and learning for all people.

Solutions

Achieving racial inclusion within educational settings requires a multifaceted approach that addresses various challenges encountered in the action stage. Overcoming cultural bias, promoting diversity in the curriculum, providing comprehensive teacher training, dismantling institutional racism, and securing sufficient resources are essential components of fostering a racially inclusive environment. Collaboration among policymakers, educators, and community stakeholders is crucial to ensure effective and sustained progress toward racial inclusion, ultimately leading to a more equitable and harmonious society. To overcome these challenges, proactive measures must be taken at all levels to reshape educational systems and create an inclusive and equitable learning environment for everyone.

Policy reforms play a vital role in promoting racial inclusion. Governments can implement affirmative action policies, anti-discrimination laws, and diversity initiatives to address systemic inequalities. This requires an inclusive approach involving input from marginalized communities, activists, and experts. By embracing policies that address racial disparities, societies can work toward creating a more inclusive and equitable environment.

Education and awareness programs are essential to combat racism and promote racial inclusion. Educational institutions should incorporate anti-racist curricula that educate students about the historical and social contexts of racial discrimination. Students can challenge biases and contribute positively to racial inclusion efforts by fostering empathy, understanding, and critical thinking. Raising awareness through campaigns, workshops, and seminars also helps dismantle stereotypes and foster intercultural understanding.

Representation in influential institutions is crucial to enhancing racial inclusion. Organizations, corporations, and government bodies should strive to diversify their leadership positions, ensuring that people from all racial backgrounds are represented. This can be achieved by implementing equity-driven hiring and promotion practices, establishing mentorship programs, and creating safe spaces for individuals to voice their concerns. Effective representation leads to better decision-making, policies, and practices catering to the diverse communities' needs.

Building inclusive communities requires active community engagement and grassroots movements. These initiatives empower individuals from marginalized groups, amplifying their voices and perspectives. Encouraging community-led initiatives, such as forums, support groups, and cultural events, fosters a sense of belonging and strengthens community bonds. Collaborating with local organizations, community leaders, and activists helps address specific racial inequalities and bring about positive change at the grassroots level.

Maintenance Stage

Once people complete the action stage, they enter the maintenance stage, which focuses on sustaining the achieved changes. Educators should encourage reflection, provide ongoing support, and address potential threats to avoid relapse or loss of motivation.

Racial inclusion refers to the systematic effort to create equitable environments where individuals from diverse racial backgrounds feel valued and respected and have equal opportunities to participate, succeed, and thrive. While significant progress has been made in advancing racial inclusion, various challenges persist in the maintenance stage of this process.

Challenges

One of the primary challenges in the maintenance stage of racial inclusion is the lack of sustained commitment from educational institutions to address systemic racism. Initiating inclusive policies and programs is commendable, but with long-term dedication and institutionalized support, ensuring equity and inclusion for students of all racial backgrounds becomes easier.

Resistance to change often emerges when institutions attempt to dismantle systemic racism. This resistance may come from various stakeholders, including staff, faculty, and students. Resistance to change can hinder the maintenance of racial inclusion efforts, causing a regression to previous discriminatory practices. Addressing this challenge requires strategic planning, open dialogue, and constructive engagement to promote understanding and progress.

Maintaining racial inclusion in the education system requires appropriate representation of diverse racial backgrounds within staff, faculty, and leadership positions. However, historically, positions of power within educational institutions have been predominantly occupied by individuals from the majority racial group. The lack of representation perpetuates systemic biases and can hinder efforts to maintain racial inclusion.

Sustaining racial inclusion requires the allocation of adequate resources, including financial support, training programs, and educational materials. However, educational institutions often face resource limitations, making it challenging to provide the necessary tools and support for ongoing racial inclusion initiatives.

Cultural insensitivity can hinder the maintenance of racial inclusion in educational settings. It involves the lack of awareness, understanding, or respect for diverse cultural practices, traditions, and values. In some cases, curriculum content may perpetuate stereotypes or disregard the contributions of racial minorities. Addressing cultural insensitivity requires ongoing training, multicultural education, and a commitment to inclusivity from all stakeholders involved in the educational process.

In the maintenance stage of racial inclusion, it is crucial to acknowledge and address the intersectionality of race with other forms of oppression, such as gender, socioeconomic status, and ability. Failure to consider the multifaceted experiences of individuals from diverse racial backgrounds can hinder efforts to maintain inclusive environments.

Solutions

Maintaining racial inclusion at the education level is a complex and ongoing process. The challenges faced in the maintenance stage include insufficient institutional commitment, resistance to change, lack of representation, inadequate resources and support, cultural insensitivity, and addressing intersectionality and multiple oppressions. Overcoming these challenges requires sustained commitment, continual learning, and collaboration among educational institutions, stakeholders, and communities. By doing so, we can create and maintain equitable educational environments where all individuals, regardless of their racial backgrounds, can thrive, succeed, and contribute to society.

One effective solution in the maintenance stage of racial inclusion is the implementation of cultural competency training for educators, administrators, and staff members. This training aims to raise awareness about cultural diversity, dismantle biases, and enable individuals to navigate and appreciate different cultural perspectives effectively. By imparting knowledge and fostering empathy, cultural competency training equips educators with the skills required to create an inclusive environment for all people, regardless of their racial backgrounds.

To ensure that inclusion efforts are effective, regular assessment and evaluation mechanisms need to be established. This involves measuring progress, identifying challenges, and making necessary adjustments. Educational institutions should collect data on student outcomes, evaluate the experiences of racially diverse people, and monitor staff and faculty engagement in promoting racial inclusion. By analyzing this information, institutions can identify gaps in their inclusivity efforts and develop targeted interventions to address them.

Mentorship and support programs play a pivotal role in the maintenance stage of racial inclusion. These initiatives can provide people from marginalized racial backgrounds with the guidance and infrastructure necessary to overcome obstacles. By pairing racially diverse students with mentors who share similar backgrounds or experiences, these programs offer a safe space for students to seek advice, enhance their skills, and develop a sense of belonging. Institutions can also create peer support networks that foster inclusivity and allow people to share their experiences, challenges, and triumphs.

To promote racial inclusion at an educational level, it is essential to incorporate diverse perspectives and histories into the curriculum. This would involve revising existing course material to include contributions from different racial backgrounds, including marginalized communities. By representing a broad range of voices, experiences, and achievements, the curriculum can challenge stereotypes, promote inclusivity, and broaden students' understanding of race-related issues. A holistic approach to racial inclusion requires collaboration with external community partners who are also invested in fostering inclusivity. Educational institutions can partner with local organizations, community leaders, and activists.

Conclusion

Racial discrimination in America has deep historical roots and originates in slavery and the Jim Crow era more than two hundred years ago. Despite efforts to combat racism, racial disparities still persist in our daily lives, such as in police shootings and incarceration rates. Understanding this history is crucial in addressing and overcoming ongoing challenges in achieving racial equality. The death of George Floyd in 2020 serves as a tragic reminder of the continued presence of racial discrimination in American society. Despite the persistent existence of racial discrimination, which plagues the physical and mental health of both BIPOC individuals and White people, now is the time to start racial trauma healing and move forward from racial discrimination to inclusiveness.

Healing from the trauma associated with racism requires a clear understanding of the definition of racism-related stress and the ways it manifests in unfair treatment and prejudices. The aim of the healing process is not to blame or accuse anyone of any racial background; instead, it is the first step to describe and heal the damages caused by racism. Racial discrimination can take various forms, from overt acts of hatred to subtle biases that perpetuate inequality. It is an issue that affects both White individuals and people of color, and avoiding the topic only allows its impact to persist.

Over the past years, racism has been prevalent in every corner of our lives, and it takes various forms of its presentation. There are multiple levels of racial discrimination, starting with individual racism, which includes discriminatory actions and biases based on race that individuals hold. Internalized racism is when individuals internalize and accept negative stereotypes about their own racial/ethnic group. Interpersonal racism occurs between individuals and includes explicit and implicit biases. Institutional racism is discrimination perpetuated by political, economic, or legal institutions and systems, such as the criminal justice system, educational institutions, and workplaces. Social and racial discrimination is a societal issue that perpetuates stereotypes and biases through media representation and lack of diversity. Cultural racial discrimination imposes norms and values as the standard, marginalizing and excluding individuals from different cultural backgrounds. These forms of racism have detrimental consequences for individuals and communities, perpetuating inequalities and hindering social cohesion.

Throughout the previous chapters, one clear conclusion is that all people (both BIPOC and White people) suffer the negative consequences of racism. However, different people experience different symptoms due to racism. Because this book discusses the consequences of racial discrimination on both BIPOC individuals and White people, this book acknowledges that BIPOC individuals experience racial traumas and trauma-related symptoms. In contrast, White people struggle with White supremacy, White privileges, White fragility, and emotional distress such as White guilt. Racial discrimination, which is a violation of human rights, continues to be prevalent in everyday life, from interpersonal interactions to policymaking. The consequences of racial discrimination for BIPOC individuals include psychological, emotional, and physical harm, as well as diminished self-worth, increased stress, anxiety, depression, and a heightened sense of vulnerability. Racial discrimination also perpetuates inequality, marginalization, social division, and tension.

This book also applies four theories to describe the impacts of racism on BIPOC. For example, with a generic stress model, Landrine and Klonoff (1996) developed SRE focusing on its frequency and intensity of race for Black individuals. In contrast, Clark et al. (1999) developed a biopsychosocial model that considers racism as a stressor for Black people. They incorporated Black individuals' perception of racism as an environmental stimulus, leading to amplified psychological and physiological stress responses. The article by Clark et al. raised four key points: (1) racism-related stress is a chronic experience for Black individuals, impacting their psychological well-being and physical health; (2) racism-related stress is detrimental to physical health and psychological well-being, inspiring future research on the harmful effects of racism; (3) the article promotes research on health disparities, highlighting the connection between racism, social environment, and health outcomes; and (4) it addresses the underrepresentation of Black individuals within academic settings. Overall, the article highlights the need to understand and address the impacts of racism on Black individuals' well-being.

Clark et al.'s (1999) article discusses four critical points on racism. Firstly, the article focuses on the chronic experience of racism for Black individuals, highlighting the effects of racial discrimination, institutional discrimination, and microaggressions. The authors argue that racism is a chronic stressor that leads to psychological distress and compromised physical health. Secondly, the article emphasizes the detrimental impact of racism on the physical health and psychological well-being of Black individuals. It calls for further research into the harmful effects of racism on physical health conditions such as heart disease and diabetes. The article also highlights disparities in healthcare facilities, access to fresh food, and fitness centers between Black and White neighborhoods. Thirdly, Clark et al. (1999) argue that their article supports the need for research on health disparities. They connect racism, social environment, and the damage caused by racism to physical health and psychological well-being. Understanding the causes and consequences of health disparities and racism is crucial for reducing these disparities and minimizing the impacts of racism.

In the past decade, the concept of racism was referred to as racial trauma and its potential to trigger symptoms of PTSD among BIPOC. It references DSM-5 criteria for PTSD and highlights the various ways in which racism can be experienced, including individual racism and institutional racism. The text also mentions a study by Carter et al. (2013) that developed a scale called the Race-Based Traumatic Stress Symptom Scale (RBTS) to assess the psychological, behavioral, and physiological impact of racism on BIPOC individuals. The RBTS recognizes the immediate and long-lasting effects of racism-related stress and aims to provide a comprehensive assessment of its impact.

Taken together, racism has been conceptualized from race-related stress to racial trauma in the past years. The evolution of defining racism from stressful events to racial trauma demonstrates the research evidence and connections that racism needs to be conceptualized to fit with BIPOC individuals' cultural and historical contexts. The consequences of racism have been addressed, from stressful experiences to symptoms aligned with the criteria in the Diagnostic and Statistical Manual of Mental Disorders (Carter et al., 2017). Aligned with PTSD in DSM-5, regarding racial trauma, it is critical to recognize both the actual experiences and perceptions of racism-related stress, as well as the intergenerational effects of historical trauma (Carter, 2007; Carter et al., 2013).

Despite various racial trauma symptoms that plague BIPOC individuals' health, Chao (in process) emphasizes the need to integrate the concept of racial trauma with the strengths and resilience of BIPOC communities to promote healing and social justice. It also explores the role of post-traumatic growth and culture-unique strengths in coping with and thriving against racial trauma (Williams et al., 2022). This book introduces Chao's model of integrating racial trauma and BIPOC's strengths as a way to understand the complexities of racial trauma, trauma healing, and BIPOC's thriving against racism-related stress. To move forward to racial inclusion, this text emphasizes the detrimental impact of racial trauma on BIPOC's well-being and health but also highlights their strengths and resilience in managing and overcoming these experiences (Chou et al., 2012).

Another conclusion from the previous chapters is that racism also damages White people's psychological and emotional health, such as denial, hearing, and guilt when some White people feel discomfort in engaging in race-related conversations. This book also addresses the damages and costs of racial discrimination against White people. Thus, this book highlights that racial discrimination not only affects BIPOC individuals but also has negative consequences for White individuals. This book addresses that racial anxieties caused by racism can lead White people to experience health concerns (Metzl, 2019). It also discusses the psychological and emotional well-being of White people, mentioning feelings of White guilt, White shame, and confusion about their identity (Chao et al., 2015; Spanierman & Heppner, 2004). The book further concludes that the impacts of White supremacy, Whiteness, White privilege, and colorblind racial attitudes on White individuals' physical health, mental well-being, relationships, and personal growth (Bonilla-Silva, 2022). The negative emotional consequences discussed include White guilt, White fragility, White shame, White fear, White fatigue, and White vulnerability (Collins & Watson, 2021). Therefore, this book confirms that racial discrimination has detrimental effects on White people's lives and well-being.

It has taken the United States more than 200 years to struggle with racism, and unfortunately, the journey is not complete yet. This process of racial trauma healing serves as a foundation for the journey from racial discrimination to racial inclusion, and the transition started with anti-racism pioneers and fighters centuries ago, though it is still ongoing. The importance of acknowledging the starting point of transformation, such as the civil rights movement, is emphasized in the previous chapters. Racial inclusion is seen as a collective transformation that requires efforts from people of all racial backgrounds. Likewise, individuals from all races/ethnicities experience positive impacts of racial inclusion. These anti-racism pioneers make the power of racial inclusion stronger. Similarly, people today must understand the historical significance of civil rights to explore the transformation from racial discrimination to inclusion.

Thus, it is inevitable to discuss the history and impact of the Jim Crow laws on education, particularly how disparities in education impact Black and other BIPOC students. The Jim Crow laws enforced racial segregation and limited resources and opportunities for Black schools and students, and such a lack of resources still occurs in HBCUs (Historically Black Colleges and Universities). To fight for equity in education for Black students is one primary step in civil rights, and it took many years of legislative changes, legal challenges, and activism, including the landmark Supreme Court case *Brown v. Board of Education* in 1954, to dismantle the Jim Crow laws and their effects on education. *Brown v. Board of Education* declared segregation in public schools unconstitutional and had far-reaching consequences for education and the broader civil rights movement. Such achievements and milestones inspired desegregation efforts and legal action against systemic injustice. The ruling marked a turning point in the fight against racial discrimination and propelled discussions about equality and justice in the United States.

Different from other documents and writings, this book examines the tragedy of the assassination of Dr. Martin Luther King Jr. from the perspective that the civil rights movement and anti-racism activities will not die after Dr. King's death. Although Dr. King's death caused shock, grief, and anger, it also sparked riots and halted progress on civil rights legislation; however, it ultimately led to a shift in the civil rights movement, with new leaders emerging and more confrontational approaches being pursued (Granberg, 1971). The assassination had a profound effect on the African American community, reinforcing the importance of ongoing efforts to combat racism and inequality. It also forced the nation to confront its deep-seated racism and highlighted the need for social change. The text also mentions the creation of the Civil Rights Division of the Department of Justice and the ongoing struggle for civil rights. It discusses the Black Power movement, the Civil Rights Act of 1964, the educational, social, economic, and legislative impacts of the Civil Rights Movement, and the increased representation of African Americans in politics. The text highlights the historical importance and lasting legacy of Dr. King's assassination and the Civil Rights Movement in the fight for equality and justice (Whitlinger & Fretwell, 2019).

This book also conceptualizes Dr. King's tragic assassination as an inspiration for anti-racism exercises such as the Blue Eyes/Brown Eyes exercise developed by Jane Elliott (Elliott, 2017). Specifically, the exercise aims to promote inclusivity and address racial discrimination by dividing participants into two groups based on eye color and attributing superiority to one group. This book also highlights the effectiveness of these anti-racism exercises in promoting critical consciousness, empathy, and understanding, challenging implicit biases, and fostering transformative learning. It also emphasizes the importance of White individuals joining the anti-racism movement in creating a more equitable society.

Besides anti-racism exercises, the transformation from racial discrimination to inclusion gets stronger with numerous White anti-racism pioneers. Thus, this book highlights four White individuals' contributions to racial inclusion and civil rights. However, we believe that there are more White anti-racist activists and pioneers not included in this book. This book highlights the contributions of Virginia Foster Durr, J. Waties, Anne McCarty

Braden, and Herbert R. Kohl. For example, Virginia Foster Durr was a civil rights activist and writer who fought against racism, sexism, and poverty. J. Waties Waring was a judge who challenged racial segregation and played a role in the desegregation of schools. Anne McCarty Braden was a civil rights activist and journalist who exposed racial inequality and fought for social justice. Herbert R. Kohl was an educator and author who promoted student-centered learning, critical pedagogy, multicultural education, and alternative teaching methods. These individuals have left a lasting impact on American society and continue to inspire activism and progress in pursuing social and racial equality.

This book also highlights several key issues that these pioneers teach us, including the importance of awareness and empathy toward the experiences of racial minorities, the moral imperative to reject racism and work toward social justice, the personal growth and healing that can come from engaging in anti-racism work, the role of White allies in supporting marginalized communities, and the importance of a diverse and inclusive movement to dismantle systemic racism effectively. It emphasizes that the involvement of White individuals in the anti-racism movement adds credibility and influence to the cause and encourages them to use their privilege to challenge discriminatory policies and advocate for racial justice.

The transformation toward racial inclusion could be challenging, emotional, and complex despite it being a collective effort by BIPOC and White individuals. This book describes the contrasting perspectives of Malcolm X's earlier experiences and Martin Luther King Jr.'s on White people and their evolution over time. Malcolm X initially harbored resentment toward White people, while Dr. King had faith in their goodness. However, Malcolm X's perspective changed after his pilgrimage to Mecca, where he encountered kind and accepting White Muslims. He began to embrace collaboration with White activists for racial equality. Malcolm X's evolving perspective emphasized the importance of building bridges between races. His example demonstrates growth and understanding. This book borrows his and Dr. King's principles to focus on compassion and empathy across races/ethnicities during the transformation process.

Because the healing of racism-related issues is essential for both BIPOC individuals and White people, this book indicates the importance and necessity of tailoring racial healing for BIPOC and White people as they experience different symptoms of racism. This book also emphasizes that racial healing goes beyond individual healing and that policies and systems must be restructured to reduce disparities. Like Nilon (2022, p. 590) mentioned, "give language to the experiences involved in the encounter," this book believes that recognizing racial trauma and identifying various sources of racial discrimination, including individual, institutional, structural, and systemic racism, opens the door to racial healing and the transformation to racial inclusion. Thus, the previous chapters identify racism in legal contexts, community voice and lived experiences, intergenerational racism, media influence and representation, historical narratives and colonial legacy, and intersectionality and multiple discrimination. Moreover, this book concludes that, instead of falling on a few people's shoulders, it is the collective responsibility of BIPOC and White people to identify and address the sources of racism to heal racial trauma and promote inclusion and justice.

After identifying and naming the sources of racism, the next step is to heal. The text discusses the concepts of racial trauma healing, trauma-informed care for racism, healing racial discrimination with mindfulness, and transforming to racial inclusion. Since it takes a collective effort to identify the sources of racism, it is also necessary to address racial trauma and dismantle systemic racism through collective efforts. The previous chapters explore transforming to racial inclusion through openness to diversity, empathy across cultures, and celebrating culture-specific strengths. Empathy toward others and oneself is highlighted as an essential tool for self-acceptance and understanding in the context of racial issues.

Without celebrating the strengths of various cultures, including BIPOC and White, the transformation journey is missing a critical part because each culture strengthens the transformation through its culture-related strengths. This book highlights the resilience, community, and artistic contributions of Black culture, the importance of family and discipline in Asian culture, the resilience and diversity of Latino/a culture, the resilience and interconnectedness with nature in American Indian culture, and the intellectual and technological advancements of White culture. This book emphasizes the importance of recognizing and appreciating different cultures' strengths while acknowledging the need for racial inclusion and equality.

Finally, this book highlights that anti-racism pedagogy is an educational approach that aims to address and dismantle institutionalized racism in education systems. It promotes inclusivity, critical thinking, empowerment of marginalized communities, cultural competence, challenging biases and stereotypes, and active citizenship. By incorporating these principles into education, anti-racism pedagogy seeks to reduce racial achievement gaps and create a more equitable educational environment.

Racial inclusion is essential and beneficial for individuals, communities, and societies. When individuals from different racial backgrounds are included and valued, they can contribute their talents and perspectives. This leads to innovation, creativity, problem-solving, economic growth, and social cohesion. Everyone deserves to experience the positive outcomes of racial inclusion.

The previous chapters explain the principles of racial inclusion, which aim to create positive outcomes for all individuals. Racial inclusion promotes social justice, reduces socioeconomic disparities, and provides equitable access to opportunities, resources, and social services. In racially inclusive societies, there are improvements in mental and physical health outcomes as individuals feel a sense of belonging, safety, and support. The fundamental principles and practices of racial inclusion include equal opportunities, diverse representation, cultural competence, non-discrimination, equitable policies, education and awareness, and community engagement. Racial inclusion is part of a broader effort to build a more just and equitable world, requiring ongoing commitment and active efforts to dismantle barriers and promote equality. The positive outcomes of racial inclusion include social equality and cohesion, empathy development, economic prosperity, and enhanced international reputation and soft power. Racial inclusion benefits marginalized communities and enriches society, fostering a more equitable, empathetic, and prosperous world.

Racial inclusion refers to creating an environment that embraces diversity and promotes equal opportunities for individuals of various racial backgrounds. Racial inclusion has multiple benefits, including personal growth, improved emotional well-being, increased understanding and empathy toward others, breaking down social barriers, and fostering innovation and collaboration. Racial inclusion also serves as a collective healing process for individuals and communities, addressing historical injustices and contributing to societal transformation. It enhances individuals' sense of belonging, fosters empathy and perspective-taking abilities, boosts cognitive abilities, and promotes resilience and multicultural competence. Racial inclusion also has emotional benefits, including an enhanced sense of belonging and identity, the development of empathy and emotional intelligence, reduced emotional stress and anxiety, and the building of harmonious community relations.

The benefits of racial inclusion at the institutional level, particularly in educational institutions and workplaces, are numerous and significant. Racial inclusion promotes equality, social justice, and a more equitable society. It leads to improved academic outcomes in educational institutions, fosters critical thinking and empathy, and promotes cross-cultural understanding. It also prepares students for diverse workplaces and contributes to personal growth. In the workplace, racial inclusion fosters diversity as a competitive advantage, enhances collaboration and teamwork, promotes innovation and creativity, and enhances employee satisfaction and retention. Embracing racial inclusion is more than a moral obligation and a strategic imperative for organizations aiming to thrive in a diverse world.

This book also discusses the benefits of racial inclusion at the systemic level because the benefits of racial inclusion go beyond the individual level.

It explains that racial inclusion promotes economic growth and innovation by tapping into a wider talent pool and stimulating entrepreneurship. Diverse teams generate better ideas, leading to higher productivity and innovation. Racial inclusion enhances problem-solving and decision-making by bringing diverse perspectives, resulting in more comprehensive solutions to complex issues. Furthermore, racial inclusion fosters social cohesion and a sense of belonging by ensuring that individuals from all racial backgrounds feel respected and embraced. This leads to stronger community bonds, reduced social tensions, and healthier communities. Additionally, racial inclusion positively impacts public health outcomes, as inclusive societies tend to have better overall health indicators.

Moreover, collaboration is the key to a successful transformation. The book also highlights the importance of collaboration on anti-racism, as it brings together individuals from different racial backgrounds to work toward equality. Collaboration harnesses the strength of diversity and leads to a comprehensive understanding of racial issues and the development of practical solutions. It also promotes cross-cultural understanding, empathy, and shared goals, fostering unity and eradicating racism. Collaboration on anti-racism is crucial for driving progress against racial injustices and achieving social harmony. Lastly, the text emphasizes that social justice and racial inclusion go hand in hand, as racial inclusion is a crucial component of social justice that ensures equitable access to resources and opportunities for individuals from diverse racial backgrounds. Increasing social justice leads to a fairer and more harmonious society, reducing disparities in education, healthcare, and overall well-being. Racial inclusion and social justice have numerous benefits, from economic advancement to improved community well-being and happiness. Achieving social justice requires continuous efforts at both individual and systemic levels, but the rewards are invaluable for creating a more equitable and just society for all.

To prevent racial inclusion from encountering potential barriers and failures, this text discusses the transformation process and the challenges faced in achieving it. The previous chapters emphasize the importance of self-awareness, setting clear goals, acquiring knowledge and skills, taking action, accountability and evaluation, and integration and consolidation. The challenges in each stage are explored, including the complexity of issues, historical context, biases, limited awareness, resistance to change, lack of resources, societal resistance, limited representation, and lack of accountability and evaluation measures. This book also suggests potential solutions, such as raising awareness, providing training and education, revising curriculum and resources, fostering dialogue and safe spaces, promoting representation, and improving accountability and evaluation methods. This book highlights the multifaceted nature of achieving racial inclusion and the need for comprehensive strategies and continuous commitment.

Following the stage of change model (Prochaska & DiClemente, 1982), this book discusses the stages of the change model in racial inclusion. The model proposes that individuals undergo stages when modifying their behavior, including pre-contemplation, contemplation, preparation, action, and maintenance (Prochaska & DiClemente, 1983). Integrating the stage of change model, this book explores each stage in the context of racial inclusion. The previous chapters identify barriers to each stage and add solutions to promote racial inclusion. Specifically, challenges in the pre-contemplation stage include historical and social factors, ignorance, and fear and resistance to change. Solutions include raising awareness, providing education, and challenging existing biases. The contemplation stage involves challenges such as a lack of understanding, resistance to change, and the sociopolitical climate. Solutions include education, awareness campaigns, and representation. When racial inclusion is in the preparation stage, we face challenges such as lack of awareness, resistance, institutional barriers, limited resources, and lack of cultural competence. Solutions include policy reforms, education and awareness programs, representation, and community engagement. The action stage encounters challenges such as cultural bias, lack of representation, insufficient teacher training, institutional racism, and limited resources. Solutions include addressing cultural bias, diversifying the curriculum, providing teacher training, addressing institutional racism, and securing adequate resources. The maintenance stage faces challenges such as insufficient institutional commitment, resistance to change, lack of representation, inadequate resources and support, cultural insensitivity, and addressing intersectionality. Solutions include cultural competency training, regular assessment and evaluation, mentorship and support programs, diverse curricula, and collaboration with external partners. Reflecting on the stage of change, it is noted that several challenges, such as fear, resistance, and lack of resources, are prevalent through different stages, while several solutions to promote education and reduce disparities appear critical in various stages.

In summary, this book presents six conclusions: (a) Racism has haunted and affected both BIPOC and White individuals. (b) The effects of racism should be understood based on individuals' cultural backgrounds. For instance, BIPOC individuals experience symptoms of racial trauma, while White individuals experience denial and other negative psychological consequences. (c) Achieving racial healing requires a collective effort, starting with identifying the sources of racism. (d) Examples of cross-racial collaborations can be observed in civil rights and anti-racism movements. (e) The transition from racial discrimination to inclusion involves various stages, each with its own challenges and solutions. (f) All individuals deserve equal opportunities and the chance to experience the benefits of racial inclusion.

References

Alston, M., Darity, W. A., Eckel, C. C., McNeil, L., & Sharpe, R. (2022). The effect of stereotypes on black college test scores at a historically black university. *Journal of Economic Behavior & Organization, 194*, 408–424. https://doi-org.du.idm.oclc.org/10.1016/j.jebo.2021.12.005

Alvarez, K., Cervantes, P. E., Nelson, K. L., Seag, D. E. M., Horwitz, S. M., & Hoagwood, K. E. (2022). Review: Structural racism, children's mental health service systems, and recommendations for policy and practice change. *Journal of the American Academy of Child & Adolescent Psychiatry, 61*(9), 1087–1105. https://doi-org.du.idm.oclc.org/10.1016/j.jaac.2021.12.006

American Psychiatric Association. (2013). *Diagnostic and statistical manual of mental disorders* (5th ed). Arlington, VA: American Psychiatric Association.

Anālayo, B. (2020). Confronting racism with mindfulness. *Mindfulness, 11*(10), 2283–2297. https://doi-org.du.idm.oclc.org/10.1007/s12671-020-01432-4

Baker, D. B., & Benjamin, L. T., Jr. (2000). The affirmation of the scientist-practitioner: A look back at Boulder. *American Psychologist, 55*(2), 241–247. https://doi-org.du.idm.oclc.org/10.1037/0003-066X.55.2.241

Baumeister, R. & Leary, M. (1995). The need to belong: Desire for interpersonal attachments as a fundamental human motivation. *Psychological Bulletin, 117*(3), 497–529. http://doi.org/10.1037/0033-2909.117.3.497

Billings, A. G., & Moos, R. (1981). The role of coping responses and social resources in attenuating the stress of life events. *Journal of Behavioral Medicine, 4*, 139–157.

Bonilla-Silva, E. (2022). *Racism without racists: Color blind racism and the persistence of racial inequality in America* (6th ed.). Lanham, MD: Rowman & Littlefield.

Bowleg, L. (2017). Intersectionality: An underutilized but essential theoretical framework for social psychology. In B. Gough (Ed.), *The Palgrave handbook of critical social psychology* (pp. 507–529). Palgrave Macmillan. https://doi.org/10.1057/978-1-137-51018-1_25

Bowleg, L. (2023). The white racial frame of public health discourses about racialized health differences and "dis-parities": What it reveals about power and how it thwarts health equity. *Frontiers in Public Health, 11*, 1187307. https://doi.org/10.3389/fpubh.2023.1187307

Braveman, P. A., Arkin, E., Proctor, D., & Holm, N. (2022). Systemic and structural racism: Definitions, examples, health damages, and approaches to dismantling. *Health Affairs, 41*(2), 171, 178.

Britannica, T. Editors of Encyclopaedia. (2024, January 7). Institutional racism. *Encyclopedia Britannica*. Retrieved March 16, 2024, from https://www.britannica.com/topic/institutional-racism

Brown, C. S. (2002). *Refusing racism: White allies and the struggle for civil rights.* New York: Teachers College Press.

Brown, C. S. (2006). Bias at school: Perceptions of racial/ethnic discrimination among Latino and European American children. *Cognitive Development, 21*(4), 401–419. https://doi.org/10.1016/j.cogdev.2006.06.006

Carter, R. T. (2007). Racism and psychological and emotional injury: Recognizing and assessing race-based traumatic stress. *The Counseling Psychologist*, *35*(1), 13–105. https://doi-org.du.idm.oclc.org/10.1177/0011000006292033

Carter, R. T., Johnson, V. E., Roberson, K., Mazzula, S. L., Kirkinis, K., & Sant-Barket, S. (2017). Race-based traumatic stress, racial identity statuses, and psychological functioning: An exploratory investigation. *Professional Psychology: Research and Practice, 48*(1), 30–37. https://doi.org/10.1037/pro0000116

Carter, R. T., Mazzula, S., Victoria, R., Vazquez, R., Hall, S., Smith, S., Sant-Barket, S., Forsyth, J., Bazelais, K., & Williams, B. (2013). Initial development of the race-based traumatic stress symptom scale: Assessing the emotional impact of racism. *Psychological Trauma: Theory, Research, Practice, and Policy*, *5*(1), 1–9. https://doi-org.du.idm.oclc.org/10.1037/a0025911

Chao, R. C.-L. (In Progress). *A model of integration of racial trauma and BIPOC's strength.*

Chao, R. C.-L., Wei, M., Spanierman, L., Longo, J., & Northart, D. (2015). White racial attitudes and White empathy: The moderation of openness to diversity. *The Counseling Psychologist*, *43*(1), 94–120. https://doi-org.du.idm.oclc.org/10.1177/0011000014546871

Chou, T., Asnaani, A., & Hofmann, S. G. (2012). Perception of racial discrimination and psychopathology across three US ethnic minority groups. *Cultural Diversity and Ethnic Minority Psychology*, *18*(1), 74–81. https://doi-org.du.idm.oclc.org/10.1037/a0025432

Clark, K. B. (1979). The role of social scientists 25 years after Brown. *Personality and Social Psychology Bulletin*, *5*(4), 477–481. https://doi-org.du.idm.oclc.org/10.1177/014616727900500408

Clark, K. B., & Clark, M. K. (1939). Segregation as a factor in the racial identification of Negro pre-school children: A preliminary report. *Journal of Experimental Education, 8,* 161–163.

Clark, R., Anderson, N. B., Clark, V. R., & Williams, D. R. (1999). Racism as a stressor for African Americans: A biopsychosocial model. *American Psychologist, 54*(10), 805–816. https://doi-org.du.idm.oclc.org/10.1037/0003-066X.54.10.805

Cokley, K. (2018). How MLK's death changed America. *Dallas News*. Retrieved March 8, 2024, from https://www.dallasnews.com/opinion/commentary/2018/03/27/how-mlk-s-death-changed-america.

Collins, C. R., & Watson, E. (2021). Subverting whiteness: A systems theoretical approach to anti-racist praxis. *Global Journal of Community Psychology Practice, 12*(3), 1–27.

Comas-Díaz, L., Hall, G. N., & Neville, H. A. (2019). Racial trauma: Theory, research, and healing: Introduction to the special issue. *American Psychologist, 74*(1), 1–5. https://doi-org.du.idm.oclc.org/10.1037/amp0000442

Comas-Díaz, L., & Jacobsen, F. M. (2024). Decolonial psychotherapy: Joining the circle, healing the wound. In L. Comas-Díaz, H. Y. Adames, & N. Y. Chavez-Dueñas (Eds.), *Decolonial psychology: Toward anticolonial theories, research, training, and practice*. (pp. 295–320). American Psychological Association. https://doi-org.du.idm.oclc.org/10.1037/0000376-013

Conner, T. (2022). Black faculty and radical retention. *Footnotes, 50*(2). Washington, DC: American Sociological Association. Retrieved March 19, 2024, from https://www.asanet.org/footnotes-article/black-faculty-and-radical-retention/

DeBlaere, C., & Moradi, B. (2008). Structures of the schedules of racist and sexist events: Confirmatory factor analyses of African American women's responses. *Psychology of Women Quarterly, 32*(1), 83–94. https://doi.org/10.1111/j.1471-6402.2007.00409.x

Department of Justice. (2000). *Federal protections against national origin discrimination*. Retrieved March 17, 2024, from https://www.justice.gov/crt/federal-protections-against-national-origin-discrimination-1

DiAngelo, R. (2018). *White fragility: Why it's so hard for White people to talk about racism*. New York: Beacon Press.

Efird, C. R., & Lightfoot, A. F. (2020). Missing mayberry: How whiteness shapes perceptions of health among white Americans in a rural Southern community. *Social Science & Medicine, 253*, 112967. https://doi.org/10.1016/j.socscimed.2020.11296

Efird, C. R., Wilkins, C. L., & Versey, H. S. (2024). Whiteness hurts society: How whiteness shapes mental, physical, and social health outcomes. *Journal of Social Issues*. https://doi-org.du.idm.oclc.org/10.1111/josi.12598

Elliott, G. (2016). *10 ways white supremacy wounds white people: A tale of mutuality*. American Friends Service Committee. Retrieved March 23, 2024, from https://afsc.org/news/10-ways-white-supremacy-wounds-white-people-tale-mutuality

Elliott, J. (2017). It's all about ignorance: Reflections from the blue-eyed/brown-eyed exercise. In C. G. Sibley & F. K. Barlow (Eds.), *The Cambridge handbook of the psychology of prejudice* (pp. 655–668). Cambridge: Cambridge University Press. https://doi-org.du.idm.oclc.org/10.1017/9781316161579.029

Ford, B. Q., Green, D. J., & Gross, J. J. (2022). White fragility: An emotion regulation perspective. *American Psychologist, 77*(4), 510–524. https://doi-org.du.idm.oclc.org/10.1037/amp0000968

Ford, C. L., Griffith, D. M., Bruce, M. A., & Gilbert, K. L. (Eds.). (2019). *Racism: Science and tools for the public health professional.* Washington, DC: American Public Health Association.

Ford, C. L., & Sharif, M. Z. (2020). Arabs, whiteness, and health disparities: The need for critical race theory and data. *American Journal of Public Health, 110*(8), e2–e3. https://doi.org/10.2105/AJPH.2020.305749

French, B. H., Lewis, J. A., Mosley, D. V., Adames, H. Y., Chavez-Dueñas, N. Y., Chen, G. A., & Neville, H. A. (2020). Toward a psychological framework of radical healing in communities of color. *The Counseling Psychologist*, *48*(1), 14–46. https://doi-org.du.idm.oclc.org/10.1177/0011000019843506

Frisby, C. M. (2024). 'And that's why we're feelin' the blues': Examining associations among internalized racism, watching TV, and depression among African Americans. *Howard Journal of Communications*, *35*(1), 56–80. https://doi-org.du.idm.oclc.org/10.1080/10646175.2023.2242308

Gaskin, D. J., Dinwiddie, G. Y., Chan, K. S., & McCleary, R. (2012). Residential segregation and disparities in health care services utilization. *Medical Care Research and Review*, *69*(2), 158–175. https://doi-org.du.idm.oclc.org/10.1177/1077558711420263

Gillborn, D. (2006). Rethinking White supremacy: Who counts in 'White World.' *Ethnicities*, *6*(3), 318–340.

Giroux, H., & McLaren, P. (1994). *Between borders: Pedagogy and the politics of cultural studies.* New York: Routledge.

Gorritz, F. (2024). Addressing elements of white supremacy in counselor education: The path forward for racial justice in the counseling field. *Counselor Education and Supervision.* https://doi-org.du.idm.oclc.org/10.1002/ceas.12297

Granberg, D. (1971). Selectivity in exposure and the effect of attitudes on judgments of the mass media coverage of the King assassination. *The Journal of Social Psychology*, *85*(1), 147–148. https://doi-org.du.idm.oclc.org/10.1080/00224545.1971.9918558

Grier-Reed, T., Maples, A., Houseworth, J., & Ajayi, A. (2023). Posttraumatic growth and flourishing in the face of racial trauma. *Psychological Trauma: Theory, Research, Practice, and Policy*, *15*(1), 37–44. https://doi-org.du.idm.oclc.org/10.1037/tra0001220.supp (Supplemental)

Grzanka, P. R., Gonzalez, K. A., & Spanierman, L. B. (2019). White supremacy and counseling psychology: A critical–conceptual framework. *The Counseling Psychologist*, *47*(4), 478–529. https://doi-org.du.idm.oclc.org/10.1177/0011000019880843

Hays, D. G., Bayne, H. B., Gay, J. L., McNiece, Z. P., & Park, C. (2023). A systematic review of Whiteness assessment properties and assumptions: Implications for counselor training and research. *Counseling Outcome Research and Evaluation, 14*(1), 58–76. https://doi-org.du.idm.oclc.org/10.1080/21501378.2021.1891877

Hipolito-Delgado, C. P. (2010). Exploring the etiology of ethnic self-hatred: Internalized racism in Chicana/o and Latina/o college students. *Journal of College Student Development*, *51*(3), 319–331. https://doi-org.du.idm.oclc.org/10.1353/csd.0.0133

Jean, P. L., Lockett, G. M., Bridges, B., & Mosley, D. V. (2023). Addressing the impact of racial trauma on Black, Indigenous, and People of Color's (BIPOC) mental, emotional, and physical health through critical consciousness and radical healing: Recommendations for mental health providers. *Current Treatment Options in Psychiatry*, *10*(4), 372–382. https://doi-org.du.idm.oclc.org/10.1007/s40501-023-00304-7

Jones, J. L., & Mehr, S. L. (2007). Foundations and assumptions of the scientist-practitioner model. *American Behavioral Scientist*, *50*(6), 766–771. https://doi-org.du.idm.oclc.org/10.1177/0002764206296454

Kenny, K. (2023). *The Problem of immigration in a slaveholding republic: Policing mobility in the nineteenth-century United States.* New York: Oxford University Press.

Keramidas, A. M. (2021). Protecting the self, protecting White supremacy: Exploring the relationship between psychological defense, gender, and White fragility [ProQuest Information & Learning]. In *Dissertation abstracts international: Section B: The sciences and engineering* (Vol. 82, Issue 12–B).

Kim, S. E., Hunt, E., Tsai, W., & Huang, C. Y. (2024). Examining racial discrimination, internalized racism, and racial–ethnic socialization among Asian American parents. *Asian American Journal of Psychology*, *15*(1), 31–41. https://doi-org.du.idm.oclc.org/10.1037/aap0000321

King, D. D., Fattoracci, E. S. M., Hollingsworth, D. W., Stahr, E., & Nelson, M. (2023). When thriving requires effortful surviving: Delineating manifestations and resource expenditure outcomes of microaggressions for Black employees. *Journal of Applied Psychology*, *108*(2), 183–207. https://doi-org.du.idm.oclc.org/10.1037/apl0001016

King, M. L., Jr. (1968a, February 4). *The drum major instinct.* Sermon at Ebenezer Baptist Church in Atlanta, Georgia.

King, M. L., Jr. (1968b). *I have a dream; the quotations of Martin Luther King Jr.* New York: Grosset.

Kochhar, R., & Moslimani, M. (2023). Wealth gaps across racial and ethnic groups. Pew Research Center. Retrieved March 23, 2024, from https://www.pewresearch.org/race-ethnicity/2023/12/04/wealth-gaps-across-racial-and-ethnic-groups/

Kohl, H. R. (1967). *36 Children.* New York: New American Library.

Kohl, H. R. (1969). The open classroom: A practical guide for teachers. New York: New York Review.

Kohl, H. R. (1991). *I won't learn from you: And other thoughts on creative maladjustment.* Minneapolis, MN: Milkweed Editions.

Kohl, H. R. (1996). *Should we burn babar? Essays on children's literature and the power of stories.* New York: The New Press.

Kornienko, O., Rambaran, J. A., & Rivas-Drake, D. (2022). Interpersonal racism and peer relationships: An integrative framework and directions for research. *Journal of Applied Developmental Psychology*, *80*, 1–14. https://doiorg.du.idm.oclc.org/10.1016/j.appdev.2022.101414

Landrine, H., & Klonoff, E. A. (1996). The schedule of racist events: A measure of racial discrimination and a study of its negative physical and mental health consequences. *Journal of Black Psychology*, *22*(2), 144–168. https://doi-org.du.idm.oclc.org/10.1177/00957984960222002

Lang, D. L. (2001). The schedule of racist events-generic: A measure of perceived racism across ethnic groups. *Dissertation Abstracts International: Section B: The Sciences and Engineering, 61*(12-B), 6756.

Lazarus, R. S. (1966). *Psychological stress and the coping process.* New York: McGraw-Hill.

Malat, J., Mayorga-Gallo, S., & Williams, D. R. (2018). The effects of whiteness on the health of whites in the USA. *Social Science & Medicine, 199*, 148–156. https://doi-org.du.idm.oclc.org/10.1016/j.socscimed.2017.06.034

Magnet, S., & Dunnington, C.-L. (2022). Emotional justice as an antidote to loneliness: Children's books, listening and connection. *Feminist Theory, 23*(1), 125–139. https://doi-org.du.idm.oclc.org/10.1177/14647001211062746

McCray, T. (2023, September 28). HBCU underfunding stretches more than a century, morgan state professor argues. *Open Campus.* Retrieved March 23, 2024, from https://capitalbnews.org/hbcu-underfunding-states-biden

McIntosh, P. (2003). White privilege: Unpacking the invisible knapsack. In S. Plous (Ed.), *Understanding prejudice and discrimination* (pp. 191–196). New York: McGraw-Hill.

Metzl, J. M. (2019). *Dying of whiteness: How the Politics of Racial Resentment Is Killing America's Heartland.* Basic Books.

Metzl, J. M., & MacLeish, K. T. (2015). Mental illness, mass shootings, and the politics of American firearms. *American Journal of Public Health, 105*(2), 240–249. https://doi-org.du.idm.oclc.org/10.2105/AJPH.2014.302242

Mullany, A., Barbieri, M., Smith, S., Gubrium, A., & Valdez, L. A. (2022). "Who is our real enemy?" Internalized racism in the Puerto Rican diaspora and the role of political education within community health intervention. *Social Science & Medicine, 311*, 1–8. https://doi-org.du.idm.oclc.org/10.1016/j.socscimed.2022.115334

Mushonga, D. R., Rasheem, S., & Anderson, D. (2021). And still I rise: Resilience factors contributing to posttraumatic growth in African American women. *Journal of Black Psychology, 47*(2–3), 151–176. https://doi-org.du.idm.oclc.org/10.1177/0095798420979805

Nazroo, J. Y., Bhui, K. S., & Rhodes, J. (2020). Where next for understanding race/ethnic inequalities in severe mental illness? Structural, interpersonal and institutional racism. *Sociology of Health & Illness, 42*(2), 262–276. https://doi-org.du.idm.oclc.org/10.1111/1467-9566.13001

NBC News. (2022). *Report: Black people are still killed by police at a higher rate than other groups.* Retrieved December 11, 2023, from https://www.nbcnews.com/news/nbcblk/report-black-people-are-still-killed-police-higher-rate-groups-rcna17169

Neblett, E. W., Jr. (2023). Racial, ethnic, and cultural resilience factors in African American youth mental health. *Annual Review of Clinical Psychology, 19*, 361–379. https://doi-org.du.idm.oclc.org/10.1146/annurev-clinpsy-072720-015146

Neblett, E. W., Jr., & Neal, A. J. (2022). Measuring institutional and structural racism in research on adolescence and developmental science. *Journal of Research on Adolescence, 32*(4), 1280–1284. https://doi-org.du.idm.oclc.org/10.1111/jora.12810

Neville, H. A., Lilly, R. L., Duran, G., Lee, R. M., & Browne, L. (2000). Construction and initial validation of the color-blind racial attitudes scale (CoBRAS). *Journal of Counseling Psychology*, *47*(1), 59–70. https://doi-org.du.idm.oclc.org/10.1037/0022-0167.47.1.59

Ng, A. C., & Chu, W. (2024). Confirmatory factor analysis of the race-based traumatic stress symptom scale in a sample of Asian American adults. *Psychological Trauma: Theory, Research, Practice, and Policy*, *16*(2), 250–253. https://doi-org.du.idm.oclc.org/10.1037/tra0001451.supp (Supplemental)

Nilon, M. J. (2022). Enacting racial healing: A prospective method and model. *Pastoral Psychology*. https://doi-org.du.idm.oclc.org/10.1007/s11089-022-01045-9

Nittle, N. K. (2021, July 31). What is the definition of internalized racism? *Thought Co.* Retrieved March 15, 2024, fom thoughtco.com/what-is-internalized-racism-2834958

Oxford University Press. (2024). *Internalized racism*. Retrieved March 15, 2024, from https://www.oxfordreference.com/display/10.1093/oi/authority.20110803100007228

Page, S. E. (2007). *The difference: How the power of diversity creates better groups, firms, schools, and societies (new edition)*. Princeton: Princeton University Press. https://doi.org/10.2307/j.ctt7sp9c

Paslay, C. (2020). *Exploring White fragility: Debating the effects of Whiteness studies on America's schools*. Lanham, MD: Rowman & Littlefield.

Pieterse, A. L., Johnson, V., & Carter, R. T. (2024). The relationship between posttraumatic stress disorder and race-based traumatic stress. *Psychological Trauma: Theory, Research, Practice, and Policy*, *16*(2), 208–216. https://doi-org.du.idm.oclc.org/10.1037/tra0001528

Poussaint A. F. (2002). Yes: It can be a delusional symptom of psychotic disorders. *The Western Journal of Medicine*, *176*(1), 4. https://doi.org/10.1136/ewjm.176.1.4

Prochaska, J. O., & DiClemente, C. C. (1982). Transtheoretical therapy: Toward a more integrative model of change. *Psychotherapy: Theory, Research & Practice*, *19*(3), 276–288. https://doi-org.du.idm.oclc.org/10.1037/h0088437

Prochaska, J. O., & DiClemente, C. C. (1983). Stages and processes of self-change of smoking: Toward an integrative model of change. *Journal of Consulting and Clinical Psychology*, *51*(3), 390–395. https://doi-org.du.idm.oclc.org/10.1037/0022-006X.51.3.390

Spanierman, L. B., & Heppner, M. J. (2004). Psychosocial costs of racism to Whites scale (PCRW): Construction and initial validation. *Journal of Counseling Psychology*, *51*(2), 249–262. https://doi-org.du.idm.oclc.org/10.1037/0022-0167.51.2.249

Thompson, C. E., & Neville, H. A. (1999). Racism, mental health, and change: Some further thoughts. *The Counseling Psychologist*, *27*(2), 256–262. https://doi-org.du.idm.oclc.org/10.1177/0011000099272005

U.S. Department of Education. (2023). *FACT SHEET: Biden-Harris administration highlights a record of championing historically black colleges and universities (HBCUs)*. https://www.ed.gov/news/press-releases/fact-sheet-biden-harris-administration-highlights-record-championing-historically-black-colleges-and-universities-hbcus. Retrieved on March 23, 2024.

Wei, M., Yeh, C. J., Chao, R. C.-L., Carrera, S., & Su, J. C. (2013). Family support, self-esteem, and perceived racial discrimination among Asian American male college students. *Journal of Counseling Psychology*, *60*(3), 453–461. https://doi-org.du.idm.oclc.org/10.1037/a0032344

Whitlinger, C., & Fretwell, J. (2019). Political assassination and social movement outcomes: Martin Luther King and the Memphis Sanitation workers' strike. *Sociological Perspectives*, *62*(4), 455–474. https://doi-org.du.idm.oclc.org/10.1177/0731121419842116

Williams, M. T., Holmes, S., Zare, M., Haeny, A., & Faber, S. (2022). An evidence-based approach for treating stress and trauma due to racism. *Cognitive and Behavioral Practice*. https://doi-org.du.idm.oclc.org/10.1016/j.cbpra.2022.07.001

Williams, W. S., Ginsberg, A., & Mandryk, B. (2016). Sociocultural contexts and stressors. In S. Maltzman (Ed.), *The Oxford handbook of treatment processes and outcomes in psychology: A multidisciplinary, biopsychosocial approach* (pp. 55–75). Oxford: Oxford University Press.

Willis, H. A., Sosoo, E. E., Bernard, D. L., Neal, A., & Neblett, E. W. (2021). The associations between internalized racism, racial identity, and psychological distress. *Emerging Adulthood*, *9*(4), 384–400. https://doi-org.du.idm.oclc.org/10.1177/21676968211005598

Wilson-Ahlstrom, A. (2018). *How racism damages us as White people*. Retrieved March 16, 2024, from https://www.debbyirving.com/how-racism-damages-us-as-white-people/

Zetzer, H. A. (2018). Whiteout: Growing out of the problem of white privilege. In S. K. Anderson & V. A. Middleton (Eds.), *Explorations in diversity: Examining the complexities of privilege, discrimination, and oppression* (3rd ed., pp. 9–24). Oxford: Oxford University Press.

Zubaran, C., Balbinotti, M., Cappelletti, K., Foresti, K., Michelin, L., & Madi, J. M. (2020). The portuguese version of the schedule of racist events. *Journal of Racial and Ethnic Health Disparities*, *7*(1), 162–168. https://doi-org.du.idm.oclc.org/10.1007/s40615-019-00645-1

Index

About the Author

Ruth Chu-Lien Chao is professor at the University of Denver, where she teaches diversity, psychopathology, counseling theories, and counseling practicum. Dr. Chao is the author of *Multicultural Competencies in Counseling: A Statistical Exploration* and *Counseling Psychology: An Integrated Positive Psychological Approach*, as well as more than 80 publications, presentations, and book chapters. She was the 2007 recipient of the American Psychological Fund Award and the American Psychological Association Grant Award. In 2005, she received the Outstanding Research Award from Division 17, APA. Dr. Chao serves as a faculty adviser to international scholars from Uzbekistan and Taiwan. Her most recent article is "Effects of a Video Intervention and Ethnocultural Empathy on Racial Color-blindness, White Empathy, and Willingness to Confront White Privilege," published in *Cultural Diversity & Ethnic Minority Psychology*.

www.ingramcontent.com/pod-product-compliance
Ingram Content Group UK Ltd.
Pitfield, Milton Keynes, MK11 3LW, UK
UKHW041839031026
15587UKWH00002B/891

9 781666 946499